GREEN REVOLUTION

GREEN REVOLUTION

Sustainable Solutions for a Healthy Planet

B. VINCENT

QuantumQuill Press

CONTENTS

Chapter 1: Introduction to the Environmental Crisis

Perceiving the Call of the Unexplored World

As the first light breaks into the great beyond, giving occasion to feel qualms about the brilliant shade of the immaculate scenes of our planet, there exists a certain charm to the obscure, coaxing us forward into unknown domains. Similar to the valiant pioneers of old who thought for even a second to wander past the recognizable limits of their guides, we end up remaining on the incline of another period—aa time characterized not by the success of far-off lands but rather by the stewardship of our own delicate planet.

Notwithstanding the ecological emergency that looms forebodingly not too far off, we are defied by the distinct truth of our interconnectedness with the normal world. The call of the obscure, once held for the gutsy individuals who tried to vanquish new wildernesses, presently reverberates inside every one of us as we wrestle with the vulnerability of what lies ahead. It is a source of inspiration, a call to leave on an excursion of revelation and recovery—an excursion that will test the constraints of our fortitude and flexibility.

However, in embracing the soul of experience, we find comfort in the information that we are in good company in this undertaking. For as we look at the huge spread of the regular world, we are helped to remember the endless species that call this planet home—every one depending on the sensitive equilibrium of environments that support life itself. It is a lowering acknowledgment—one that urges us to adapt to the situation before us and to face the natural vulnerabilities that take steps to disentangle the texture of life as far as we might be concerned.

In any case, in the midst of the vulnerability, there exists a promise of something better—aa reference point of light that guides us forward on our excursion. The feeling of miracle mixes inside us, lighting a flash of interest and wonder for our general surroundings. Despite affliction, it is our capacity to wonder about the magnificence and intricacy of the normal world that supports our soul and energizes our assurance to persist.

So let us regard the call of the obscure as embracing the soul of experience that exists in every one of us. Allow us to set out to investigate new skylines, to stir things up, and to fashion a way towards a more maintainable future. For it is in embracing the obscure that we find the genuine degree of our solidarity and flexibility—the characteristics that will convey us forward on our excursion towards a better, more energetic planet.

Confronting Ecological Vulnerabilities

In the maze of ecological difficulties that defies us, vulnerability rules—an imposing enemy that tests the actual texture of our purpose. Like mariners exploring misleading waters, we end up wrestling with the consistently moving flows of environmental change, the inauspicious phantom of biodiversity misfortune, and the tricky killjoy of contamination. Despite such vulnerability, it is normal to feel a feeling of trepidation, a chewing dread of the obscure that takes steps to deaden us in our tracks.

However, it is unequivocally in snapshots of vulnerability that our actual strength is uncovered. For it is just when we defy the obscure with boldness and versatility that we can outline a course towards a more promising time to come. Similarly, as wayfarers of old overcame the unfamiliar oceans looking for new grounds, so too should we bring the boldness to stand up to the ecological vulnerabilities that lie before us.

It is an overwhelming undertaking, no doubt—one that expects us to explore a mind-boggling trap of interrelated difficulties with no way forward. In any case, in dealing with these vulnerabilities directly, we find a repository of solidarity and versatility inside ourselves that we never knew existed. It is an update that difficulty, a long way from being an obstacle, is much of the time the impetus for development and change.

As we go up against the natural vulnerabilities that lie before us, it is fundamental that we do so with modesty and elegance. We should recognize the restrictions of our insight and embrace the chance of disappointment as a chance for learning and development. For it is simply by embracing vulnerability that we can genuinely improve and adjust, notwithstanding change.

So let us face the ecological vulnerabilities that lie before us with mental fortitude and assurance. Allow us to embrace the obscure as a chance for development and change instead of a boundary to advance. For it is in defying vulnerability that we find the genuine degree of our solidarity and strength—the characteristics that will convey us forward on our excursion towards a better, more supportable future.

Developing a feeling of miracle

In the buzzing about of present-day life, it is really quite simple to become disengaged from the regular world that encompasses us

—to fail to focus on the sensational magnificence and intricacy that lie just past our doorstep. However, it is precisely in snapshots of quietness and reflection that we are helped to remember the significant interconnectedness of every living thing and the mind-boggling snare of life that supports us.

Developing a feeling of miracle isn't only an extravagance, but also a need—aa fundamental counteractant to the unresponsiveness and lack of concern that frequently go with the everyday routine. It is an update that we are nevertheless one little string in the rich embroidery of life—aa woven artwork woven together by endless ages of plants, creatures, and environments, each assuming a novel and indispensable part.

At the point when we get some margin to stop and really notice the regular world around us, we are met with a kaleidoscope of sights, sounds, and vibes that never neglect to dazzle the creative mind. From the fragile dance of a butterfly on the breeze to the great glory of a transcending redwood tree, each experience fills in as a delicate sign of the marvel and magnificence that lie at the core of our reality.

Yet, developing a feeling of wonder is something beyond a practice in care—it is a source of inspiration and an impetus for change. When we reconnect with the regular world on a more profound level, we can't resist the urge to feel an awareness of certain expectations to safeguard and protect them for people in the future. It is an acknowledgment that our destinies are entwined with the destiny of the actual planet—that in focusing on the earth, we care for ourselves.

So let us take a second to stride outside, to take in the natural air, and to wonder about the marvels that encompass us. Allow us to revive the feeling of miracle that lies lethargic inside every one of us, and let it act as a directing light on our excursion towards a more reasonable and amicable relationship with the normal world.

For it is in developing a feeling of marvel that we find the genuine lavishness and excellence of life itself—an extravagance that merits safeguarding no matter what.

Embracing Development and Innovation

Despite overwhelming natural difficulties, it turns out to be progressively apparent that customary methodologies alone won't get the job done. It is here, in the midst of the tumult and vulnerability, that development and imagination arise as our most powerful partners, offering new viewpoints, novel arrangements, and strange pathways towards a more reasonable future.

Embracing development expects us to throw away assumptions and embrace the obscure with a receptive outlook and a readiness to investigate the neglected. It is a call to break free from the bounds of show, to rock the boat, and to really hope for an existence where manageability isn't simply a yearning but a reality.

At its center, advancement is about something beyond the improvement of new innovations or the execution of novel methodologies—it is about generally rethinking our relationship with the normal world. It is tied in with tracking down motivation in the complex examples of nature and saddling the force of biomimicry to plan arrangements that are powerful yet agreeable with the environments that support us.

Imagination, as well, assumes an essential part in the excursion towards maintainability. The flash lights the blazes of advancement, driving us to consider new ideas and really pause for a moment to think about additional opportunities where others see just snags. Whether it be through artistic expression, the sciences, or the humanities, imagination has the ability to move, inspire, and catalyze change on a worldwide scale.

Yet, advancement and inventiveness are not without their difficulties. They expect us to embrace disappointment as an unavoidable piece of the inventive approach and to endure even with affliction. They request persistence, diligence, and a readiness to learn from our errors—an eagerness to repeat, adjust, and develop as we endeavor towards our objectives.

So let us embrace development and inventiveness as our core values on the excursion towards a more practical future. Allow us to really hope for an existence where humankind resides as one with nature, and let us work enthusiastically to carry that fantasy to completion. For it is in embracing development and imagination that we open the endless capability of human creativity and prepare for a more splendid and practical tomorrow.

Heading Out Towards Reasonable Arrangements

With the breeze at our backs and the stars as our aid, we stand on the cliff of another sunrise—aa day break that guarantees not simply the continuation of life as far as we might be concerned, but the chance of a more brilliant, more feasible future for all. As we leave on this excursion towards manageability, it is fundamental that we set our sights solidly, not too far off, and diagram a course that leads us towards our common objectives.

Heading out towards reasonable arrangements requires a diverse methodology—one that envelops mechanical development yet also social, monetary, and social change. An excursion requests joint effort, collaboration, and aggregate activity on a worldwide scale—an acknowledgment that the difficulties we face are excessively perfect for any one individual or country to defeat alone.

At the core of our journey for manageability lies a guarantee of stewardship—to really focus on the earth and every one of its occupants with the very love and regard that we would show towards our own home. It is an acknowledgment that we are nevertheless impermanent caretakers of this planet and that it is our obligation to leave it in a preferred state over time so we can track it down for people in the future.

Yet, heading out towards manageable arrangements isn't just about moderating the harm we have proactively done; it is likewise about jumping all over the chance to fabricate a superior world for all. It is tied in with rethinking our urban areas as energetic center points of advancement and imagination, our economies as motors of maintainable development, and our social orders as guides to civil rights and equity.

As we explore the dubious waters that lie ahead, let us draw motivation from the endless ages of travelers who have preceded us—gutsy people who really considered wandering into the obscure looking for new terrains and additional opportunities. Allow us to tackle the forces of development, imagination, and cooperation to chart a course towards a future where humankind resides as one with nature and where the fantasies of a supportable tomorrow turn into a reality.

Chapter 2: Understanding Climate Change

Clarification of Environmental Change Causes

Inside the many-sided embroidery of Earth's natural frameworks, a peculiarity of extraordinary importance has started to disentangle—the consistent walk of environmental change. At its center, environmental change is driven by a complicated interaction of variables, each adding to the sensitive equilibrium between our planet's climate and biological systems. As we dive into the profundities of this part, we leave on an excursion to disentangle the secrets of environmental change, starting with an investigation of its principal causes.

Integral to the comprehension of environmental change lies the peculiarity of ozone-depleting substance emanations, a result of human activities like consuming non-renewable energy sources, deforestation, and modern cycles. These emanations, essentially carbon dioxide, methane, and nitrous oxide, go about as a cover, catching intensity inside Earth's climate and prompting the continuous warming of the planet—aa cycle known as the nursery impact.

In any case, the narrative of environmental change isn't exclusively bound to the domain of ozone-harming substances. Without a doubt, other human activities, for example, land-use changes, urbanization, and farming, likewise assume a huge part in molding the world's environmental framework. Deforestation, for instance, not only diminishes the limit of backwoods to retain carbon dioxide, but in addition adds to the deficiency of biodiversity and the debasement of biological systems—aa blade that cuts both ways with broad results.

As we disentangle the unpredictable trap of causality behind environmental change, it turns out to be progressively certain that human activities are at the core of this worldwide test. The consuming of non-renewable energy sources to control our enterprises, the getting free from timberlands to clear a path for farming, and the tenacious quest for monetary development no matter what—every one of these exercises demands a cost for the planet, pushing us nearer and nearer to the edge of fiasco.

In any case, in the midst of despair and vulnerability, there exists a good omen—an acknowledgment that, on the off chance that humankind is equipped for driving environmental change, without a doubt we have the ability to switch its course. It is a source of inspiration—aa revitalizing sob for people, networks, and countries to meet up in quest for a shared objective: to face the main drivers of environmental change and to fashion a way towards a more practical and versatile future for all.

Effects of Environmental Change

As the wheels of modern advancement keep on turning, the resonations of human movement reverberate a long way past the bounds of our urban communities and production lines, molding the actual texture of our planet's biological systems and scenes. No place are these resonations more definitely felt than in the domain of environmental change—aa peculiarity whose effects stretch out from the most elevated tops to the most profound sea channels, leaving no edge of the globe immaculate.

At the core of the environmental change story lies a reiteration of desperate outcomes, each a demonstration of the significant disturbance created within the world's regular frameworks. Climbing worldwide temperatures, driven by the collection of ozone-depleting substances in the environment, have gotten rolling with a fountain of impacts, from the dissolution of polar ice covers and glacial masses to the fermentation of our seas—an unmistakable sign of the delicacy of the planet's fragile balance.

In any case, the effects of environmental change are not restricted to the domain of the normal world. For sure, human social orders are additionally feeling the strain as outrageous climate occasions become more continuous and more serious, disturbing livelihoods, uprooting networks, and compounding social disparities. From dry seasons and out-of-control fires to typhoons and floods, the fingerprints of environmental change are indisputable—aa harbinger of a future laden with vulnerability and commotion.

However, in the midst of the mayhem and despondency, there exists a promising sign—an acknowledgment that, assuming we act quickly and conclusively, we can, in any case, deflect the most terrible effects of environmental change and fabricate a stronger future for a long time into the future. It is an invitation to battle—aa revitalizing sob for aggregate activity and fortitude notwithstanding difficulty. For while the difficulties before us might be overwhelming, they are not impossible—not assuming that we bring the boldness and assurance to defy them head-on.

So let us regard the alerts of the normal world and act with criticalness to address the effects of environmental change. Allow us to embrace the chance to fashion another way—one characterized not by annihilation and misery but rather by strength, advancement, and trust. For it is in standing up to the effects of environmental change that we find the genuine degree of our solidarity and flexibility—the characteristics that will convey us forward on our excursion towards an additional feasible and impartial future.

Alleviation Systems

Even with the approaching phantom of environmental change, mankind winds up at a basic intersection—aa point where the choices we make today will shape the direction of our planet for a long time into the future. However, in the midst of the vulnerability and desperation existing apart from everything else, there exists a good omen—an acknowledgment that, assuming we act conclusively and with reason, we can in any case guide the course of history towards an additional practical and strong future.

At the core of our reaction to environmental change lies a set-up of moderation methodologies—activities pointed toward decreasing the emanation of ozone-harming substances and restricting the degree of an Earth-wide temperature boost. These systems span a large number of areas and disciplines, from energy and transportation to farming and land use, and each holds the possibility of having a huge effect in our battle against environmental change.

Vital to any successful alleviation methodology is the progress away from petroleum products towards perfect, sustainable wellsprings of energy, for example, sunlight-based, wind-based, and hydropower. By saddling the force of the sun, the breeze, and the world's regular assets, we can not just lessen our reliance on limited and contaminating petroleum derivatives but, in addition, set out new open doors for financial development and improvement.

However, the way to a low-carbon future isn't without its difficulties. It requires striking authority, aggressive targets, and exceptional degrees of participation and cooperation among countries and partners. It likewise requests a readiness to stand up to dug-in interests and vested businesses that might try to protect the norm at any expense.

However, in the midst of the hindrances and vulnerabilities, there exists an abundance of chance—an opportunity to fabricate a world that isn't just cleaner and greener, but also more impartial and just. It is an opportunity to put resources into new innovations, make green positions, and enable networks to assume command over their own predeterminations. It is an opportunity to produce another common agreement—one that places the necessities of individuals and the planet above transient benefits and personal matters.

So let us jump all over this chance with two hands and set out on an excursion towards an additional, maintainable, and versatile future. Allow us to embrace the test of environmental change as an impetus for positive change—an opportunity to reconsider our relationship with the normal world and construct a world that genuinely deserves people in the future. For it is in facing the difficulties of today that we lay the foundation for a more splendid tomorrow —aa tomorrow where the commitment of a manageable and even-handed future turns into a reality.

Transformation Techniques

As the persistent walk of environmental change proceeds unabated, humankind winds up faced with a critical goal: to adjust to the quickly moving real factors of our planet's environmental framework. From the burning heatwaves that dry the land to the downpours of rain that immerse our urban communities, the effects of environmental change are now being felt all over, leaving no edge of the globe immaculate.

Even with such difficulties, variation becomes a need, however, a step-by-step process for surviving—aa method for protecting our networks, economies, and biological systems against the devastation of an evolving environment. Variation systems include a wide cluster of measures, from supporting foundations and fortifying debacle readiness to improving water the board rehearses and advancing environmental versatility.

Integral to any viable transformation technique is the acknowledgement that environmental change effects will be felt lopsidedly, with weak networks and underestimated populations enduring the worst part of the weight. Thusly, variation endeavors should be directed by standards of value, equity, and inclusivity, guaranteeing that those generally impacted by environmental change are given the help and assets they need to flourish in an impacting world.

In any case, transformation isn't just about building seawalls or establishing safe dry season yields; it is likewise about embracing a better approach to thinking, one that focuses on adaptability, development, and flexibility despite vulnerability. It is tied in with perceiving that the future will be molded by the powers of nature, yet in addition by our aggregate reaction to those powers—aa reaction established in coordinated effort, collaboration, and fortitude.

As we set out on the excursion of variation, let us draw motivation from the strength of the normal world, where life has flourished and advanced notwithstanding innumerable difficulties and disturbances. Allow us to gain insight from the insights of native people groups and conventional information holders, who have managed the land for ages with love and care. What's more, let us concede to building a future where all can thrive, no matter what the difficulties that lie ahead.

Eventually, variation isn't just about getting by; it is tied in with flourishing. It is tied to embracing change as a chance for development and change and producing a way towards a more economical and tough future for all. So let us adapt to the situation before us with mental fortitude and assurance, knowing that together we have the ability to beat even the best of hindrances.

Source of inspiration

Even with the existential danger presented by environmental change, there can be no space for smugness and no time for wavering. The ideal opportunity for activity is currently. As we stand at the cliff of another period, the destiny of our planet remains in a precarious situation, wavering on the edge of calamity. In any case, in the midst of the bedlam and vulnerability, there exists a good omen—an opportunity to reverse the situation and to chart another course towards an additional reasonable and strong future.

Be that as it may, this future isn't ensured. It will require strong administration, aggressive targets, and exceptional degrees of participation and joint effort among countries and partners. It will request penances and hard decisions as we face the settled interests and vested enterprises that look to protect the state of affairs at any expense. Furthermore, it will require a central change in our outlook —an acknowledgment that the quest for momentary benefits and tight personal matters should be subjected to the long-term benefit of humankind and the planet.

Be that as it may, the awards for activity are inconceivable. By finding conclusive ways to moderate and adjust to environmental change, we might not just shield our networks and biological systems against the most terrible effects of an Earth-wide temperature boost at any point, but in addition set out new open doors for financial development, civil rights, and ecological stewardship. We can fabricate an existence where clean air and water are the inheritance of each and every resident, where green positions and maintainable innovations drive flourishing, and where the commitment of a more promising time to come is accessible for all.

So let us adapt to the situation before us with mental fortitude and assurance. Allow us to regard the admonitions of science and act with earnestness to address the underlying drivers of environmental change. Allow us to embrace the valuable chance to fabricate a future that truly deserves people in the future—one characterized not by obliteration and misery but rather by flexibility, development, and trust. For it is in facing the difficulties of today that we lay the foundation for a more splendid tomorrow—aa tomorrow where the commitment of a maintainable and fair future turns into a reality.

Chapter 3: The Role of Artificial Intelligence in Education

Grasping manageable agribusiness

In the rambling territory of our cutting-edge rural scene, where monocultures rule huge areas of land and compound data sources soak up the dirt, a calm unrest is in progress—one that tries to reconsider our relationship with the land and the food it produces. At the core of this unrest lies the idea of reasonable horticulture—an all-encompassing way to deal with cultivating that endeavors to adjust the requirements of individuals, planet, and benefit.

At its center, practical farming is grounded in a profound regard for the normal frameworks that support all life on the planet. It perceives that solid soils, clean water, and biodiversity are extravagances to be protected, but they are fundamental parts of a strong and useful rural framework. It likewise recognizes the interconnectedness of every living thing, from the organisms in the dirt to the birds overhead, and looks to develop an agreeable connection among people and the normal world.

Be that as it may, practical horticulture isn't just about natural stewardship; it is likewise about guaranteeing the drawn-out suitability of cultivating as a vocation and a lifestyle. It perceives the significance of financial supportability, guaranteeing that ranchers get fair pay for their work and speculations and that provincial networks approach the assets and foundation they need to flourish.

Maybe, in particular, feasible farming is about value and civil rights. It perceives that admittance to sound, nutritious food is a principal common freedom and that the advantages of rural improvement ought to be shared impartially among all citizens. It tries to enable limited-scope ranchers, ladies, native people groups, and other underestimated gatherings to partake completely in the rural economy and to have a voice in forming the fate of food and cultivating.

As we dig further into the standards and practices of manageable agribusiness, we start to see the significant change that is conceivable when we adjust our activities to the rhythms of nature and the necessities of people in the future. It is an excursion of revelation, of experimentation, of gaining insight from the past and the developments of the present. Yet, most importantly, it is an excursion of trust—aa conviction that by cooperating, we can fabricate a food framework that feeds the two individuals and the planet, presently and for a long time into the future.

Economical Cultivating Methods

In the verdant embroidery of our rural scenes, a variety of cultivating methods have arisen—each a demonstration of mankind's creativity and versatility, even with changing natural and social circumstances. At the bleeding edge of this mosaic lies an assortment of practices referred to on the whole as economical cultivating methods—aa set-up of approaches that look to harness the force of nature to create food while limiting damage to the planet.

One of the foundations of economical cultivation is natural farming, which shuns manufactured pesticides, composts, and hereditarily adjusted life forms for regular sources of information and practices that advance soil wellbeing and biodiversity. By sustaining the perplexing snare of life that exists underneath our feet, natural ranchers can deliver nutritious, tasty harvests while limiting adverse consequences for the climate and human wellbeing.

One more mainstay of supportable cultivating is agroforestry, a training that incorporates trees and bushes into rural frameworks to provide a range of environmental, monetary, and social advantages. By consolidating food crops with trees that give shade, asylum, and natural surroundings for untamed life, agroforestry ranchers can upgrade soil richness, moderate water, and sequester carbon—all while broadening their pay and further developing flexibility to environmental change.

Permaculture is one more way to deal with maintainable cultivation that draws motivation from normal environments to plan human settlements and rural frameworks that are both useful and regenerative. By impersonating the examples and cycles tracked down in nature, permaculture specialists can make self-supporting food backwoods, water-productive gardens, and shut-circle frameworks that limit squander and amplify asset use effectiveness.

And afterward, there is regenerative horticulture, an all-encompassing way to deal with cultivating that tries to reestablish and improve the soundness of biological systems while at the same time creating food. By zeroing in on practices, for example, cover editing, crop turning, and all-encompassing brushing, regenerative ranchers can assemble soil natural matter, further develop water penetration, and increment biodiversity—all while sequestering carbon and relieving the effects of environmental change.

As we investigate the rich embroidery of practical cultivating procedures, obviously there is no one-size-fits-all answer to the difficulties confronting horticulture today. All things being equal, there exists a range of approaches, each with its own assets and shortcomings, its own chances, and its own requirements. In any case, in the midst of this variety, there is an ongoing idea—aa common obligation to build a food framework that sustains the two individuals and the planet, presently and for a long time into the future.

Advancements in Innovation and Cultivating Strategies

In the steadily developing scene of horticulture, development has arisen as a main thrust, moving ranchers towards more noteworthy effectiveness, efficiency, and manageability. At the convergence of innovation and cultivation lie a heap of noteworthy developments that guarantee to upset the manner in which we develop, collect, and circulate food while limiting our effect on the climate.

One such development is accuracy horticulture, a set-up of innovations that influence information, sensors, and computerization to streamline each part of the cultivating system. By unequivocally observing soil dampness, supplement levels, and harvest wellbeing, accuracy agribusiness empowers ranchers to go with information-driven choices that augment yields while limiting data sources like water, compost, and pesticides. From robots and satellites that give ongoing symbolism to yield fields to GPS-directed work vehicles that can plant and collect with pinpoint accuracy, horticulture offers ranchers remarkable command over their tasks and the capacity to limit squander and ecological effect.

Tank-farming and vertical cultivating address one more boondock in rural development, offering a practical option in contrast to conventional soil-based cultivating strategies. By developing harvests in supplement-rich water arrangements and stacking them in an upward direction in environment-controlled conditions, aquaculture and vertical homesteads can deliver significant returns with negligible land and water use. These advances hold specific commitments for metropolitan regions, where land is scarce and populations are developing, offering the possibility to bring new, privately developed produce to networks all year.

Biotechnology and hereditary design likewise assume a significant role in progressing economical farming, offering the possibility to foster yields that are stronger against bugs, sicknesses, and natural burdens. From dry spell open-minded maize and irritation-safe cotton to infection-safe papaya and nutrient-advanced rice, biotech crops hold the commitment of expanding yields, lessening the requirement for synthetic information sources, and working on the dietary nature of food—all while limiting ecological effects.

As we tackle the force of development to address the difficulties confronting horticulture today, it is fundamental that we do so with a sharp eye towards supportability. While innovation offers unimaginable chances to further develop proficiency and efficiency, it likewise brings risks and potentially negative side effects that should be painstakingly considered. By embracing an all-encompassing way to deal with development—one that thinks about the social, ecological, and monetary effects of new innovations—we can fabricate a future where horticulture flourishes and where the planet thrives for a long time into the future.

Advancing Agroecological Approaches

In the midst of the commotion of present-day horticultural practices, there exists a reliable insight that harkens back to the foundations of human progress—aa comprehension that the soundness of our food frameworks is unpredictably entwined with the strength of the environments that help them. This shrewdness tracks down articulation in the standards of agroecology, a comprehensive way to deal with cultivating that looks to emulate the flexibility and variety of normal biological systems while delivering food reasonably.

At its pith, agroecology is a marriage of nature and horticulture —an acknowledgment that the ranch isn't simply a position of creation but rather a mind-boggling environment by its own doing.

By noticing and grasping the connections between plants, animals, and microorganisms, agroecologists can configure cultivating frameworks that outfit the environmental cycles of supplement cycling, bother guidelines, and soil fruitfulness to create food in a manner that is regenerative and strong.

Vital to the act of agroecology is the idea of biodiversity—the possibility that a different cluster of plants, creatures, and microorganisms is fundamental for the wellbeing and efficiency of farming frameworks. By establishing assorted crop blends, consolidating cover crops, and creating an environment for advantageous bugs and untamed life, agroecologists can incorporate strength into their cultivating frameworks, lessening the requirement for compound sources of information and relieving the effects of nuisances, illnesses, and outrageous climate occasions.

Agroecology likewise puts areas of strength on the significance of neighborhood information and local area contribution in the plan and the executives of horticultural frameworks. By drawing on the insight of native people groups, conventional ranchers, and nearby networks, agroecologists can fit their practices to the particular requirements and states of the spots where they work, guaranteeing that cultivating isn't just naturally economical yet additionally socially and socially significant.

As we dive further into the standards and practices of agroecology, obviously this approach offers a pathway towards a more supportable and evenhanded food framework—one that sustains the two individuals and planet while regarding the insight of the past and the requirements of people in the future. By embracing the standards of variety, versatility, and local area, we can fabricate a future where farming flourishes, biological systems prosper, and food is a wellspring of wellbeing, happiness, and association for all.

Strategy and Market Mediations for Maintainable Farming

In the perplexing trap of worldwide food frameworks, the choices made by policymakers and market entertainers have a tremendous impact, forming the direction of horticulture and deciding the destiny of millions of ranchers and purchasers all over the planet. Perceiving the dire need to change towards more feasible and versatile food frameworks, policymakers and market entertainers are progressively directing their concentration toward mediations that advance manageable horticulture rehearsals.

One such mediation is the execution of approaches that boost and support the reception of manageable cultivating rehearses. From endowments for natural farming and protection programs that elevate soil wellbeing to guidelines that limit the utilization of unsafe pesticides and manures, states play an urgent part in establishing an empowering climate for manageable horticulture. By adjusting horticultural strategies to ecological and social objectives, policymakers can urge ranchers to embrace rehearsals that safeguard regular assets, moderate environmental change, and advance biodiversity while guaranteeing the drawn-out reasonability of agrarian jobs.

Market mediations likewise assume a basic role in driving the progress towards economical horticulture. Buyer interest in economically delivered food is on the ascent, driven by a growing consciousness of the ecological and social effects of regular cultivating practices. Thus, retailers, food organizations, and confirmation bodies are progressively taking on manageability norms and names that signify to buyers that their items are created in a socially and naturally mindful way. By making market motivators for supportable horticulture, these mediations can drive interest in maintainable cultivating practices, empower advancement, and award ranchers for their stewardship of the land.

Simultaneously, it is fundamental that policymakers and market entertainers stay watchful to guarantee that mediations intended to advance reasonable horticulture don't incidentally propagate imbalances or compound existing social and natural treacheries. Measures should be taken to guarantee that limited-scale ranchers, ladies, native people groups, and other underestimated bunches have equivalent access to assets, markets, and dynamic cycles. Furthermore, endeavors ought to be made to address underlying obstructions and power uneven characters that block the reception of feasible horticulture rehearsals by those most out of luck.

As we explore the intricate territory of agrarian strategy and market elements, it is fundamental that we stay guided by standards of value, equity, and maintainability. By cooperating to establish an empowering climate for manageable horticulture, we can construct a future where food is created as one with nature, where ranchers flourish, and where networks are supported and engaged to shape their own fates.

Chapter 4: Renewable Energy: Powering the Future Sustainably

Prologue to environmentally friendly power sources

In the unfathomable spread of our universe, where the sun radiates brilliantly, the breeze areas of strength for blows, and the Earth beats with geothermal energy, lies the way to opening a future fueled by manageability and flexibility. At the core of this vision lies sustainable power—an encouraging sign in the battle against environmental change, ecological corruption, and energy weakness.

Environmentally friendly power sources, in contrast to their limited partners, are derived from normally recharging assets that are boundless on human timescales. From the brilliant energy of the sun and the dynamic power of the breeze to the gravitational draw of streaming water and the intensity stewing underneath the world's exterior, sustainable power offers an abundance of perfect, bountiful, and harmless options for the ecosystem in contrast to petroleum products.

At the front of the environmentally friendly power upset stands sun-oriented power—an innovation that tackles the energy of the sun to create power and intensity. Using photovoltaic cells and sun-oriented warm gatherers, sun-based energy frameworks catch daylight and convert it into usable energy, providing a dependable and feasible wellspring of force for homes, organizations, and networks all over the planet.

In any case, sunlight-based energy is only one piece of the puzzle. Wind power, as well, holds colossal commitment as a spotless and plentiful wellspring of power. By saddling the dynamic energy of moving air using wind turbines, wind ranches can deliver huge amounts of sustainable power, dislodging carbon-serious petroleum derivatives and decreasing ozone-harming substance discharges simultaneously.

Hydroelectric power, in the meantime, takes advantage of the regular progression of water to create power, tackling the gravitational possible energy of waterways and streams to turn turbines and produce spotless, sustainable power. While enormous-scope hydroelectric activities have confronted analysis for their natural and social effects, more limited-size, decentralized hydroelectric frameworks offer the potential for a feasible energy age with insignificant disturbance to environments and networks.

Geothermal energy, derived from the intensity put away underneath the world's surface, addresses one more wilderness in sustainable power improvement. By taking advantage of geothermal repositories and outfitting heat from the world's inside, geothermal power plants can create power and give warming and cooling to homes, organizations, and modern offices, offering a dependable and practical wellspring of energy with insignificant natural effect.

Lastly, there is biomass energy—aa flexible and sustainable asset made from natural materials like wood, farming buildups, and biofuels. By saddling the energy put away in biomass through cycles like ignition, gasification, and anaerobic processing, biomass energy frameworks can deliver intensity, power, and transportation energizers, offering an adaptable and sustainable option in contrast to petroleum derivatives.

As we leave on the excursion towards a future controlled by environmentally friendly power, it is fundamental that we perceive the groundbreaking capability of these innovations to reshape our energy scene and construct a more manageable and versatile world for people in the future. By bridling the force of the sun, the breeze, the water, and the actual Earth, we can make a future where energy is plentiful, clean, and open to all—aa future where mankind resides as one with the normal world instead of taking advantage of it for momentary increase.

Outfitting Sunlight-Based Energy

In the immense spread of our universe, the brilliant shine of the sun remains a timeless demonstration of the vast energy that encompasses us. Sun-based power, derived from the boundless combination of responses happening inside the sun, offers an encouraging sign as we continue looking for maintainable energy arrangements. Through the inventive organization of photovoltaic cells and sun-oriented warm frameworks, mankind has opened the possibility to saddle this bountiful energy source and change it into a perfect, sustainable power supply.

Photovoltaic (PV) innovation, the foundation of sun-oriented energy transformation, utilizes semiconductor materials to convert sunlight into power straightforwardly. As photons from the sun strike the outer layer of PV cells, they oust electrons, producing an electric flow that can be saddled for a heap of uses. From roof-sunlight-powered chargers embellishing homes and organizations to rambling sun-based ranches traversing huge spans of desert territory, PV innovation offers a flexible and versatile answer for the power age, fit for meeting the energy needs of both metropolitan and country networks.

Supplementing PV innovation is the imaginative use of sun-based warm frameworks, which outfit the intensity energy of daylight to deliver power and give warming to private, business, and modern purposes. Concentrated sun-based power (CSP) plants use mirrors or focal points to concentrate daylight onto a focal beneficiary, where it is utilized to warm a functioning liquid like water or liquid salt. This warmed liquid then, at that point, drives a turbine to produce power, offering a solid and dispatchable wellspring of sunlight-based power that can be coordinated into existing energy lattices.

In the past power age, sun-oriented energy holds massive potential for meeting an extensive variety of energy needs, from warming and cooling structures to driving transportation and desalinating water. Sun-based water warming frameworks, for instance, use sun-powered authorities to ingest daylight and intensity water for home-grown or modern use, offering an energy-efficient and practical option in contrast to regular water warming strategies. Essentially, sun-oriented controlled vehicles, going from electric vehicles to sun-based fueled boats and planes, offer a supportable method for transportation that lessens dependence on non-renewable energy sources and mitigates ozone-depleting substance discharges.

As we tackle the force of the sun to meet our energy needs, it is fundamental that we do so with a sharp eye towards manageability and value. By putting resources into a sunlight-based energy foundation, advancing innovative work, and executing steady strategies and motivating forces, we can speed up the progress towards a sun-oriented, fueled future—aa future where energy is bountiful, clean, and open to all, and where humankind lives as one with the normal world.

Taking advantage of wind power

In the tremendous fields of our air, the unending development of air murmurs a story of undiscovered capacity—aa story of wind power, a power as old as time itself, ready to be saddled to improve mankind. Wind energy, derived from the motor energy of moving air masses, remains a demonstration of our capacity to outfit the powers of nature and change them into a spotless, sustainable wellspring of power.

At the core of wind power lies the breeze turbine—aa wonder of design that catches the energy of the breeze and converts it into mechanical power. As the breeze streams over the edges of a turbine, it makes them pivot, driving a generator that produces power. From transcending coastal turbines specking the scenes of wind-rich locales to seaward wind ranches outfitting the strong whirlwinds vast ocean, wind energy offers a versatile and supportable answer for meeting our developing energy needs.

The development of wind power lately has been absolutely striking, with establishments extending quickly across the globe. Nations like China, the US, and Germany have emerged as pioneers in wind energy organization, outfitting the force of the breeze to decrease dependence on petroleum derivatives and moderate environmental change. As innovation proceeds to progress and economies of scale drive down costs, wind energy has become more serious than ordinary energy sources, offering a reasonable and harmless alternative to the ecosystem elective for the power age.

Yet, the advantages of wind power reach out in a way that makes it impossible for it to create power. Wind energy additionally offers critical natural benefits, including the decrease of ozone-harming substance emanations, the preservation of water assets, and the assurance of environments and untamed living spaces. By uprooting carbon-escalated petroleum products and lessening air and water contamination, wind power assists with moderating the effects of environmental change and further developing air quality, prompting better and more practical networks.

As we tap into the force of the breeze to meet our energy needs, it is fundamental that we do so mindfully and reasonably. This requires cautious preparation and thought of the ecological and social effects of wind energy improvement, remembering the likely impacts on natural life, scenes, and nearby networks. By drawing in partners, directing careful ecological evaluations, and carrying out prescribed procedures in siting and activity, we can guarantee that breeze energy projects are created in a way that expands benefits and limits risks for all partners included.

Eventually, wind power will address a method for creating power as well as a pathway towards a more practical and versatile energy future. By bridling the force of the breeze, we can lessen our dependence on limited and dirty petroleum products, moderate the effects of environmental change, and fabricate a reality where energy is perfect, bountiful, and open to all.

Opening Hydroelectric Potential

In the constant dance of water, from the peaceful progression of streams to the booming thunder of cascades, lies a wellspring of energy ready to be tackled—aa wellspring known as hydroelectric power. Apart from the gravitational expected energy of streaming water, hydroelectricity remains one of the most established and solid types of sustainable power, offering a perfect, plentiful, and interminably inexhaustible wellspring of power.

At the core of the hydroelectric power age lie hydroelectric dams, structures intended to catch the energy of streaming water and convert it into electrical power. As water is let out of a repository behind the dam, it courses through turbines situated at the foundation of the design, making them twist and drive generators that produce power. From enormous dams crossing the expansiveness of strong waterways to limited-scope run-of-stream projects settled in far-off valleys, hydroelectric power offers a flexible and versatile answer for meeting the energy needs of networks all over the planet.

The historical backdrop of hydroelectric power is a demonstration of humankind's capacity to tackle the force of nature for its own advantage. From the development of the Hoover Dam in the US to the Three Canyons Dam in China, hydroelectric activities have reshaped scenes, energized monetary turns of events, and given power to a great many individuals around the world. However, the advantages of hydroelectric power extend far beyond the power age, including an extensive variety of ecological, social, and monetary benefits.

One of the vital ecological advantages of hydroelectric power is its capacity to create power with negligible ozone-harming substance discharges, assisting with moderating the effects of environmental change and diminishing air contamination. By uprooting carbon-concentrated petroleum products, for example, coal and flammable gas, hydroelectricity assumes a vital role in decarbonizing the energy area and changing to a low-carbon economy. Moreover, hydroelectric dams can offer important types of assistance, for example, flood control, water systems, and water supply, assisting with overseeing water assets and backing rural and metropolitan turn of events.

However, hydroelectric power isn't without its difficulties and contentions. Huge-scope hydroelectric undertakings can have critical natural and social effects, including the disturbance of environments, the dislodging of networks, and the deficiency of social legacy locales. Accordingly, it is fundamental that hydroelectric improvement be embraced with cautious thought of the likely dangers and advantages and that endeavors be made to alleviate adverse consequences and guarantee that impacted networks are sufficiently counseled and redressed.

As we open up the capability of hydroelectricity to meet our energy needs, it is fundamental that we do so in a way that is feasible, impartial, and conscious of the regular world. By saddling the force of streaming water mindfully and sensibly, we can construct a future where energy is perfect, bountiful, and open to all, and where humankind lives as one with the waterways and streams that support life on the planet.

Investigating geothermal and biomass energy

In the midst of the profundities of the Earth and the extravagance of our backwoods lies a secret mother lode of energy ready to be tapped—aa gold mine known as geothermal and biomass energy. Given the intensity of the world's inside and the natural matter of plants and trees, these environmentally friendly power sources offer a promising pathway towards a more maintainable and tough energy future.

Geothermal energy, brought into the world from the liquid center of our planet, addresses an immense and undiscovered asset ready to be outfitted. By penetrating deeply into the world's hull, we can take advantage of supplies of high-temperature water and steam, tackling their energy to produce power and give warming and cooling to homes, organizations, and modern offices. From geothermal power plants bridling the intensity of volcanic locales to geothermal intensity siphons giving effective warming and cooling to structures, geothermal energy offers a dependable and harmless wellspring of energy with insignificant fossil fuel byproducts and ecological effects.

Be that as it may, the advantages of geothermal energy reach far beyond the power age and warming. Geothermal assets can likewise be utilized for many modern and horticultural applications, including nursery warming, hydroponics, and mineral extraction. By utilizing the intensity put away underneath our feet, we can open an abundance of chances for a supportable turn of events and monetary development, making our position and flourishing while at the same time decreasing our reliance on non-renewable energy sources and moderating environmental change.

Additionally, biomass energy uses the energy put away in natural materials like wood, horticultural deposits, and biofuels to deliver intensity, power, and transportation energy. By consuming biomass in power plants or changing it into fluid or vaporous fills, we can produce energy while at the same time decreasing waste and reusing supplements once more in the dirt. From customary biomass cookstoves utilized in rustic networks to current biomass power plants and biofuel treatment facilities, biomass energy offers a flexible and inexhaustible option in contrast to petroleum products, assisting with relieving environmental change and advancing a manageable turn of events.

Be that as it may, the supportable utilization of biomass energy requires cautious thought of its ecological and social effects, including the preservation of backwoods and normal territories, the insurance of biodiversity, and the fair dissemination of advantages and weights among partners. By advancing maintainable ranger service works, safeguarding basic environments, and supporting local area-driven biomass projects, we can guarantee that biomass energy adds to a more reasonable and evenhanded energy future for all.

As we investigate the capability of geothermal and biomass energy to meet our energy needs, it is fundamental that we do so with a sharp eye towards manageability and value. By tackling the intensity of the Earth and the force of natural matter mindfully and sensibly, we can construct a future where energy is spotless, plentiful, and open to all, and where humankind lives as one with the normal world.

Chapter 5: Conservation and Biodiversity Preservation

Grasping Protection and Biodiversity

In the multifaceted embroidery of life that covers our planet, biodiversity rules as nature's show-stopper—an ensemble of endless animal categories, each assuming a fundamental part in the working of environments and the food of life itself. Protection—the craftsmanship and study of saving this valuable variety of life—remains an encouraging sign despite mounting ecological difficulties and speeding up species eradications.

At its center, protection is an acknowledgment of the inborn worth of nature and the basic need to defend it for people in the future. It is a guarantee to safeguard the trap of life that supports us, from the glorious woods and clearing savannas to the overflowing coral reefs and clamoring metropolitan biological systems. Yet, preservation isn't just about saving scenes and territories; it is likewise about safeguarding the horde of plants, creatures, and microorganisms that call these spots home, guaranteeing that they get an opportunity to flourish and develop in an impactful world.

Biodiversity, the assortment of life on the planet, is the groundwork of preservation endeavors, filling in as both the object of security and the proportion of accomplishment. From the smallest organisms to the biggest vertebrates, each species assumes a unique role in keeping up with biological system capability and strength, adding to cycles like fertilization, seed dispersal, supplement cycling, and irritation control. In that capacity, saving biodiversity isn't simply an ethical goal; it is likewise fundamental for human prosperity, giving us clean air and water, rich soils, and the unrefined components for food, medication, and a safe house.

However, the significance of preservation extends beyond the domain of nature; it additionally incorporates social, social, and financial aspects. For the majority of networks all over the planet, especially native people groups and customary social orders, nature isn't simply a wellspring of business—it is a sacrosanct legacy, saturated with profound social importance. By safeguarding biodiversity and the biological systems that support it, we honor the inborn worth of nature as well as the privileges and customs of individuals who rely upon it for their endurance and prosperity.

As we dive further into the standards and practices of protection, we start to see the significant interconnectedness of all life on the planet—an acknowledgment that our destinies are interlaced with those of the incalculable species with whom we share this planet. Despite mounting ecological dangers and speeding up species eliminations, preservation offers us a pathway towards a more practical and agreeable relationship with the regular world—one where biodiversity flourishes, environments thrive, and mankind lives in harmony with nature.

Dangers to Biodiversity

In the sensitive equilibrium of nature, dangers to biodiversity pose a potential threat, creating a shaded area of vulnerability over the fate of life on the planet. From the widespread obliteration of regular environments to the deceptive spread of intrusive species, from the weakening impacts of environmental change to the constant abuse of natural life and assets, the powers exhibited against biodiversity protection are various, complex, and interconnected.

Territory misfortune remains one of the essential drivers of biodiversity decline, driven by human activities like deforestation, urbanization, and horticultural development. As timberlands are cleared, wetlands are depleted, and fields are changed over completely to croplands, innumerable species are driven to the edge of annihilation, denied the homes and assets they need to make due. Discontinuity of territories further mixes the issue, disengaging populaces and diminishing hereditary variety, making them more defenseless against intimidations, for example, illness and environmental change.

Environmental change addresses one more existential danger to biodiversity, disturbing biological systems and modifying the conveyance and wealth of species all over the planet. Increasing temperatures, moving precipitation examples, and more incessant outrageous climate occasions are unleashing destruction on biological systems, driving species to relocate, adjust, or die. Coral reefs, mangrove woods, and polar environments are especially powerless, confronting blanching, disintegration, and loss of living space as sea temperatures climb and ice covers liquefy.

Contamination, both earthly and oceanic, presents one more critical danger to biodiversity, debasing air, water, and soil with poisonous synthetic compounds and side effects. Pesticides, herbicides, and modern contamination poison untamed life and disturb natural cycles, while plastic contamination gags marine life and stops up streams. The multiplication of microplastics, drugs, and other arising impurities further compounds the issue, undermining the wellbeing and endurance of species from the littlest microscopic fish to the biggest whales.

Obtrusive species, presented purposefully or unintentionally by human activities, represent an unavoidable and developing danger to biodiversity, outcompeting local species, disturbing biological systems, and spreading infections. From obtrusive plants and creatures to microorganisms and parasites, intrusive species can unleash ruin on biological systems, causing decreases in biodiversity and driving local species termination. Globalization and expanded exchange have worked with the spread of intrusive species all over the planet, making them perhaps the best tests confronting protection endeavors today.

At long last, overexploitation of untamed life and regular assets represents a critical danger to biodiversity, driven by human interest in food, fuel, medication, and other items. Overfishing, poaching, and unlawful logging are annihilating populations of notorious species like elephants, rhinos, and tigers, while unreasonable gathering of plants and creatures compromises environments and livelihoods all over the planet. Unreasonable utilization examples and populace development fuel the issue, putting expanding tension on regular assets and driving biodiversity misfortune at an exceptional rate.

As we go up against the threats to biodiversity, it is fundamental that we perceive the interconnectedness of these threats and make a definitive move to address them. By securing and reestablishing living spaces, battling environmental change, lessening contamination, controlling intrusive species, and advancing economic assets as the executives rehearse, we can shield biodiversity and guarantee a sound and strong planet for people in the future.

Protection Systems and Practices

In the midst of the heap of dangers to biodiversity, a hint of something to look forward to arises—aa signal of flexibility and assurance notwithstanding misfortune. Protection systems and practices, brought into the world from the aggregate insight and creativity of researchers, policymakers, and networks all over the planet, offer a pathway towards safeguarding biodiversity and reestablishing corrupted environments. From safeguarded regions and environmental reclamation to species protection programs and the supportable assets the executives drive, these endeavors address a demonstration of our obligation to defend the snare of life that supports every one of us.

Integral to preservation endeavors is the foundation and board of safeguarded regions—regions put away to save biodiversity, safeguard normal and social legacy, and give open doors to logical examination and training. From public parks and untamed life stores to marine safeguarded regions and native domains, safeguarded regions act as imperative shelters for species and biological systems, giving places of refuge where nature can flourish undisturbed by human activities. Through viable administration and authorization of guidelines, safeguarded regions can assist with saving biodiversity, reestablishing environments, and advancing manageable improvement to support present and future generations.

Territory rebuilding addresses one more key system for saving biodiversity, pointed toward fixing and reviving environments that have been debased or obliterated by human activities. By reestablishing local vegetation, once again introducing cornerstone species, and carrying out natural surroundings the board rehearses, protectionists can assist with reproducing sound and versatile biological systems that give environment to untamed life, sequester carbon, and manage water streams. From reforestation and wetland rebuilding to seaside rise adjustment and riverbank recovery, living space reclamation endeavors offer an unmistakable and powerful method for switching the tide of biodiversity misfortune and reestablishing the soundness of corrupted scenes.

Species preservation programs assume a significant role in securing and reestablishing populations of undermined and imperiled species, guaranteeing that they get an opportunity to recuperate and flourish in their regular living spaces. Through hostage reproducing and renewed introduction programs, territory insurance and reclamation endeavors, and state-funded training and effort drives, moderates can assist with saving species from the edge of annihilation and secure their future endurance. From famous megafauna, for example, elephants and tigers, to cloud plants and bugs, each species assumes a crucial role in keeping up with environmental capability and flexibility, making species protection a foundation of biodiversity safeguarding endeavors.

Reasonable Assets: The executives address one more fundamental part of preservation endeavors, pointing toward guaranteeing that regular assets are utilized in a way that keeps up with their efficiency and trustworthiness for people in the future. By advancing reasonable fishing works, controlling logging and mining exercises, and executing supportable farming and ranger service rehearsals, preservationists can assist with limiting the effects of human activities on biological systems and biodiversity. Through cooperative methodologies that connect with nearby networks, native people groups, and partners in dynamic cycles, the economic asset the board drives can cultivate stewardship of regular assets and advance concurrence among individuals and nature.

As we embrace the difficulties and chances of protection, it is fundamental that we do so with modesty, compassion, and a profound regard for the complex trap of life that supports all of us. By cooperating to safeguard and reestablish biological systems, preserve species, and advance feasible assets as the board rehearses, we can fabricate a future where biodiversity flourishes, environments thrive, and humankind lives as one with the normal world.

Local Area Inclusion and Native Information

In the mosaic of protection endeavors, one string stands out as especially dynamic and fundamental: the contribution of neighborhood networks and the mix of native information. For centuries, native people groups and neighborhood networks have lived together as one with nature, creating mind-boggling frameworks of information, practices, and convictions that economically oversee biological systems and save biodiversity. Their profound association with the land and close comprehension of its rhythms and examples offer important experiences and viewpoints that can illuminate and upgrade preservation endeavors all over the planet.

At the core of local area associations in preservation lies the acknowledgement that neighborhood networks are not only partners in protection; they are their stewards, overseers, and champions. From native clans in the Amazon rainforest to rustic networks in the African savannas, nearby individuals have a significant stake in the wellbeing and prosperity of their scenes, depending on them for food, water, a safe house, and profound sustenance. By including these networks in dynamic cycles, engaging them with the apparatuses and assets they need to deal with their regular assets economically, and regarding their freedoms and customary information, moderates can outfit their ability and obligation to accomplish enduring and significant protection results.

Native information, sharpened through ages of lived insight and perception, offers an abundance of bits of knowledge into the biological elements of environments and the mind-boggling connections between species. From conventional land management practices, for example, agroforestry and rotational brushing, to restorative plant information and biological schedules, native information frameworks give significant illustrations on the most proficient method to live as one with nature and adjust to changing ecological circumstances. By incorporating native information into preservation planning and the board, progressives can take advantage of hundreds of years of aggregated shrewdness and upgrade the viability and pertinence of their endeavors.

Be that as it may, the contribution of nearby networks and the incorporation of native information into preservation endeavors are not simply an issue of reasonableness; they are likewise a question of equity and value. Generally underestimated and disappointed, native people groups and nearby networks frequently endure the worst part of natural corruption and biodiversity misfortune, yet their voices and points of view are habitually ignored in preservation dynamic cycles. By focusing their freedoms, necessities, and goals in preservation endeavors, we can cultivate more prominent value, inclusivity, and equity in our way of dealing with safeguarding biodiversity and advancing supportable turns of events.

As we set out on the excursion of preservation, it is fundamental that we do so with modesty, regard, and an eagerness to tune in and gain from the people who have lived as one with nature for quite a long time. By embracing the mastery and points of view of native people groups and nearby networks, we can fashion associations that honor the variety of life on the planet and guarantee that protection endeavors are established in equity, value, and regard for all creatures.

Strategy Structures and Global Participation

In the worldwide journey to defend biodiversity and save the complex embroidery of life on the planet, strategy structures and global collaboration stand as mainstays of solidarity and fortitude, directing our aggregate endeavors towards a maintainable and strong future. Perceiving the transboundary idea of ecological difficulties and the interconnectedness of biological systems and species across borders, countries all over the planet have met up to foster multilateral arrangements, settlements, and shows pointed toward safeguarding biodiversity and advancing feasible turns of events.

At the forefront of global endeavors to moderate biodiversity stands the Show on Organic Variety (CBD), a milestone settlement embraced at the Earth Culmination in Rio de Janeiro in 1992. With almost 200 member nations, the CBD addresses the most extensive worldwide settlement on biodiversity preservation, defining aggressive objectives and focusing on the protection and supportable utilization of natural variety and the fair and impartial sharing of its advantages. Through its different conventions and drives, remembering the Nagoya Convention for Access and Advantage Sharing and the Aichi Biodiversity Focuses, the CBD gives structure to activity and collaboration at the global, provincial, and public levels.

Notwithstanding the CBD, a bunch of other multilateral ecological arrangements and drives add to the worldwide protection plan, resolving explicit issues, for example, environmental change, marine biodiversity, and natural life dealing. The Unified Countries Structure Show on Environmental Change (UNFCCC), for instance, looks to address the main drivers of environmental change and advance transformation and alleviation measures to defend biological systems and biodiversity. The Show on Global Exchange Imperiled Types of Wild Fauna and Vegetation (refers to), in the mean time, plans to direct worldwide exchange jeopardized species and guarantee their endurance in nature.

However, powerful protection requires something other than the reception of peaceful accords; it additionally requires significant execution and implementation at the public and nearby levels. By coordinating biodiversity preservation into public advancement plans, arrangements, and regulations, nations can guarantee that protection targets are mainstreamed across areas and that the fundamental assets and impetuses are given to help protection endeavors. What's more, by advancing public mindfulness, schooling, and support, legislatures can encourage a culture of preservation and engage residents to make a move to safeguard biodiversity in their networks.

Global participation and cooperation are likewise fundamental for addressing transboundary dangers to biodiversity and advancing the feasible administration of shared assets. Through drives, for example, provincial preservation arrangements, cross-line safeguarded regions, and joint examination and observing projects, nations can cooperate to address normal difficulties and accomplish shared protection objectives. By pooling assets, aptitude, and political will, countries can conquer obstructions to participation and produce organizations that advance harmony, dependability, and manageability across borders.

As we explore the intricate landscape of worldwide protection, it is fundamental that we stay guided by the standards of value, equity, and supportability. By cooperating to execute and fortify peaceful accords, standard biodiversity protection into public strategies and plans, and cultivating participation and joint effort across borders, we can fabricate a future where biodiversity flourishes, environments thrive, and mankind lives as one with the regular world.

Chapter 6: Sustainable Cities and Communities

Prologue to the Practical Metropolitan Turn of Events

In the clamoring roads and transcending high rises of our cutting-edge urban areas, a dream of maintainability entices—aa dream of urban communities and networks that flourish as well as fit with the normal world, encouraging thriving, value, and flexibility for all. The economic metropolitan turn of events at its center encapsulates this vision, offering an all-encompassing way to deal with city planning and the board that tries to adjust the necessities of individuals, the planet, and people in the future.

At the core of practical metropolitan improvement lies an acknowledgment of the interconnectedness of natural, social, and financial difficulties confronting urban areas and networks around the world. From air and water contamination to gridlock and social imbalance, the effects of unreasonable urbanization are sweeping and significant, presenting existential dangers to human wellbeing, prosperity, and the respectability of biological systems. By embracing the standards of manageability—value, flexibility, and asset productivity—urban areas can transform themselves into energetic, reasonable spaces that upgrade the personal satisfaction of occupants while limiting their environmental impression.

Key to the idea of manageable metropolitan advancement is the thought of savvy, comprehensive, and incorporated arranging. By embracing a drawn-out viewpoint and taking into account the social, financial, and ecological components of improvement, urban communities can plan and carry out approaches and methodologies that advance adjusted development and manageable urbanization. From minimal, blended use improvements that diminish spread and elevate walkability to green foundation projects that upgrade flexibility and biodiversity, reasonable metropolitan preparation and configuration offer a guide for making urban communities that are bearable as well as regenerative and comprehensive.

Yet, practical metropolitan advancement isn't just about the actual foundation and plan; it is additionally about encouraging dynamic, comprehensive, and versatile networks that engage individuals to flourish. By advancing social union, social variety, and city commitment, urban areas can create spaces where occupants feel a sense of having a place and proprietorship, encouraging social capital and local area flexibility even with change and vulnerability. From people-group nurseries and recreational areas to social celebrations and neighborhood affiliations, feasible urban communities offer an abundance of chances for individuals to interface, team up, and add to the benefit of everyone.

As we set out on the excursion of manageable metropolitan turns of events, it is fundamental that we do so with a need to get a move on, desire, and aggregate reason. By embracing development, joint effort, and intense initiative, urban areas and networks can prepare for a future where urbanization isn't a wellspring of emergency and struggle but instead an impetus for positive change. In the words of urbanist Jane Jacobs, "Urban areas have the capacity of giving something to everyone, simply because, and just when, they are made by everyone." Through our aggregate endeavors, we can fabricate urban communities and networks that are reasonable as well as evenhanded, comprehensive, and versatile—urban communities that act as encouraging signs and motivation for a long time into the future.

Standards of Economical Metropolitan Preparation and Plan

Inside the maze of metropolitan scenes, an outline for reasonable metropolitan preparation and configuration arises—aa diagram established in rules that focus on ecological stewardship, social value, and monetary flourishing. Feasible metropolitan preparation and configuration offer a system for molding urban areas and networks that are ecologically tough as well as socially comprehensive and financially energetic, cultivating an amicable connection among people and the constructed climate.

Integral to practical metropolitan preparation and configuration is the conservative turn of events, which tries to limit never-ending suburbia and advance productive land use designs. By moving advancement into denser, blended-use areas and deterring spread into lacking regions, urban areas can decrease the biological impression of urbanization, safeguard normal environments and horticultural terrains, and limit the requirement for car reliance. Smaller improvements likewise elevate walkability and access to conveniences, encouraging energetic metropolitan communities where inhabitants can reside, work, and play in close proximity, decreasing dependence on vehicles, and advancing better, more dynamic ways of life.

Blended land use addresses one more key standard of maintainable metropolitan preparation and configuration: planning to make assorted, dynamic neighborhoods where private, business, and sporting activities coincide agreeably. By coordinating different land uses within a similar region, urban areas can diminish travel distances, advance social cooperation, and set out open doors for financial events and social trade. Blended use areas offer different advantages, from lessening gridlock and air contamination to encouraging a feeling of local area and having a place, making spots where individuals of any age and foundations can flourish.

A green framework assumes a basic role in maintainable metropolitan preparation and configuration, giving fundamental biological system benefits and upgrading the flexibility and decency of urban areas and networks. From metropolitan stops and green spaces to green rooftops and downpour gardens, green foundations assist with alleviating the effects of environmental change, decreasing metropolitan intensity island impacts, further developing air and water quality, and supporting biodiversity. By integrating nature into the metropolitan texture, urban areas can create better, stronger conditions that benefit both individuals and the planet.

Dynamic transportation addresses a foundation of practical metropolitan preparation and configuration, advancing strolling, cycling, and public travel as feasible options in contrast to vehicle travel. By putting resources into passerby amicable frameworks like walkways, crosswalks, and bicycle paths, urban areas can empower dynamic methods of transportation and lessen dependence on autos, subsequently decreasing gridlock, air contamination, and ozone-harming substance outflows. Public travel frameworks likewise assume an urgent role in feasible metropolitan versatility, giving reasonable, proficient options in contrast to private vehicle proprietorship and elevating evenhanded admittance to transportation administrations for all occupants.

At last, feasible metropolitan preparation and configuration focus on friendly value and inclusivity, guaranteeing that the advantages of metropolitan advancement are shared impartially among all citizens. By connecting with networks in the arranging system, consolidating different points of view and needs, and resolving issues of reasonableness, openness, and civil rights, urban communities can establish conditions that are comprehensive, tough, and engaging for all occupants. From reasonable lodging and local area offices to work-preparing projects and social administrations, economical urban communities focus on the prosperity and thriving of their residents, cultivating a feeling of having a place and a chance for all.

Maintainable Transportation and Versatility

In the musicality of metropolitan life, the beat of reasonable transportation beats consistently—an orchestra of strolling feet, turning wheels, and murmuring motors that gets individuals and merchandise across urban areas and networks while limiting natural effect. Reasonable transportation and portability address a change in perspective in metropolitan preparation and configuration, under-scoring openness, productivity, and ecological stewardship as major standards for molding transportation frameworks that address the issues of the present and people in the future.

At the core of economical transportation lies the advancement of public travel frameworks as the foundation of metropolitan ver-satility. From transports and trains to cable cars and ships, public travel offers a manageable option in contrast to private vehicle travel, giving effective, reasonable, and open transportation choices for oc-cupants and guests the same. By putting resources into great public travel frameworks and administrations, urban areas can decrease gridlock, air contamination, and ozone-depleting substance emana-tions while likewise advancing social value and upgrading versatility for underserved networks.

Cycling addresses one more foundation of maintainable metro-politan versatility, offering a spotless, sound, and productive method of transportation for short- to medium-distance trips. By putting resources into a cycling framework like bicycle paths and ways and leaving offices, urban communities can empower cycling as a reasonable option in contrast to vehicle travel, advancing active work, lessening gridlock, and further developing air quality. Cycling additionally offers various advantages for general wellbeing, including a decreased hazard of constant sicknesses like weight, diabetes, and cardiovascular infection, making it a fundamental part of reasonable transportation techniques.

A person-on foot well-disposed plan is one more key component of economical transportation and versatility, intending to make protected, agreeable, and appealing strolling conditions for inhabitants and guests. By putting resources into walker frameworks like walkways, crosswalks, and passerby courts, urban communities can energize strolling as a method of transportation and advance dynamic, walkable neighborhoods where individuals can reside, work, and play without the requirement for vehicles. The Walker amicable plan additionally cultivates social connection, local area attachment, and public wellbeing, making spaces where individuals of any age and capacity can move openly and autonomously.

The zap of transportation addresses an extraordinary chance for urban communities to decrease their carbon footprint and progress to cleaner, more manageable energy sources. Electric vehicles (EVs), controlled by sustainable power, offer a promising option in contrast to ordinary gas and diesel vehicles, giving zero-discharge transportation choices to occupants and organizations. By putting resources into an EV framework, for example, charging stations and impetuses for electric vehicle reception, urban areas can speed up the progress to electric portability and lessen air contamination, ozone-harming substance outflows, and reliance on non-renewable energy sources.

At last, reasonable transportation and versatility focus on the idea of portability as a service (Maas), which looks to incorporate different transportation choices into consistent, multimodal networks that meet the assorted requirements of explorers. From ride-sharing and carpooling to bicycle sharing and on-request travel administrations, Maas stages offer advantageous, adaptable, and effective ways for individuals to get around urban areas and networks without the requirement for private vehicle possession. By advancing Maas arrangements and cultivating coordinated effort among public and confidential transportation suppliers, urban communities can make more feasible, open, and impartial transportation frameworks that serve the requirements of all inhabitants and add to the wellbeing, flourishing, and essentialness of metropolitan life.

Economic Foundation and Asset The board

Inside the structure of reasonable urban communities and networks, the idea of framework rises above simple blocks and mortar —it envelops a dream of frameworks and designs that address the issues of the present as well as protect the assets and biological systems upon which people in the future depend. Economical framework and asset: the board addresses a principal mainstay of metropolitan supportability, offering pathways towards versatile, productive, and regenerative metropolitan conditions that flourish together as one with the normal world.

Environmentally friendly power remains a foundation for a feasible framework, offering urban areas and networks a spotless, dependable, and bountiful wellspring of force for meeting their energy needs. From solar and wind power to hydroelectric and geothermal, environmentally friendly power innovations offer versatile and financially savvy options in contrast to non-renewable energy sources, diminishing ozone-depleting substance outflows, air contamination, and reliance on limited assets. By putting resources into environmentally friendly power frameworks like sunlight-based chargers, wind turbines, and energy stockpiling frameworks, urban areas can harness the force of nature to control homes, organizations, and transportation frameworks, making more practical and versatile energy frameworks for all.

Water protection and the executives address one more fundamental part of a feasible foundation and asset for the board, especially notwithstanding the expanding water shortage and environmental inconstancy. By carrying out water-saving advancements and practices, for example, low-stream installations, water gathering frameworks, and wastewater reusing, urban areas can decrease water utilization, limit contamination, and improve resilience to dry spells and floods. Practical water for the executives likewise includes securing and reestablishing regular water frameworks like streams, wetlands, and springs, safeguarding biodiversity and environmental administrations, and guaranteeing a dependable stockpile of clean water for people in the future.

Squandering the executives is one more basic part of a supportable framework, tending to the difficulties of waste age, removal, and reusing in metropolitan conditions. By embracing systems like waste decrease, reuse, and reusing, urban areas can limit how much waste is shipped off landfills and incinerators, saving assets and diminishing contamination. Practical waste administration likewise includes advancing roundabout economy standards, where waste is seen as an important asset to be recuperated, reused, and reused, setting out monetary open doors and diminishing natural effects.

Green structures and reasonable plan rehearsals assume a crucial role in molding the constructed climate and lessening the ecological impression of urban communities and networks. By consolidating energy-efficient innovations, aloof plan systems, and manageable materials into building development and redesign projects, urban communities can lessen energy utilization, further develop indoor air quality, and lower working expenses for occupants and organizations. Green structure additionally elevates versatility to environmental change and outrageous climate occasions, improving the sturdiness and life span of structures and frameworks while making them better and more open to living spaces for tenants.

Incorporated metropolitan preparation and configuration approaches are fundamental for understanding the maximum capacity of the economic framework and assets on the board, guaranteeing that foundation speculations are composed and lined up with more extensive manageability objectives. By taking on comprehensive, framework-arranged ways to deal with foundation arranging and independent direction, urban areas can enhance asset use, limit natural effects, and boost social, monetary, and ecological advantages for all occupants. Through cooperative associations and participatory cycles, urban areas can draw in partners, cultivate advancement, and assemble agreement around manageable foundation arrangements that improve the personal satisfaction and prosperity of metropolitan networks now and into what's in store.

Local area commitment and social value

At the core of reasonable urban communities and networks lies a promise to incorporation, interest, and civil rights—an acknowledgment that the advantages of metropolitan improvement should be shared impartially among all inhabitants, paying little mind to race, identity, orientation, pay, or economic wellbeing. Local area commitment and social value address basic standards of reasonable metropolitan turn of events, offering pathways towards all the more versatile and flourishing urban communities where each voice is heard and each individual has the chance to thrive.

Local area commitment is fundamental to guaranteeing that metropolitan improvement choices are informed by the necessities, desires, and needs of neighborhood inhabitants and partners. By including networks in the preparation, planning, and execution of tasks and drives, urban communities can assemble trust, encourage joint effort, and create spaces where various viewpoints are esteemed and regarded. Local area commitment cycles can take many forms, from public gatherings and studios to participatory planning and resident-driven drives, giving open doors to inhabitants to contribute their insight, aptitude, and lived encounters to the dynamic interaction.

Social value is a major rule of the economic metropolitan turn of events, guaranteeing that the advantages and weights of urbanization are disseminated reasonably and evenhandedly among all citizens. By tending to foundational imbalances and shameful acts, urban communities can establish conditions where everybody approaches fundamental administrations, assets, and valuable open doors expected to flourish. Social value includes advancing reasonable lodging, medical care, training, and transportation choices for all occupants, as well as tending to aberrations in pay, riches, and admittance to public labor and products. It additionally involves advancing variety, inclusivity, and social ability in metropolitan preparation and dynamic cycles, guaranteeing that the necessities and viewpoints of minimized and underrepresented networks are given due thought.

Impartial access to assets and administrations is fundamental for advancing social consideration and guaranteeing that nobody is abandoned in the excursion towards a feasible metropolitan turn of events. By putting resources into reasonable lodging, medical services, schooling, and transportation choices, urban communities can establish conditions where everybody has the chance to reside, work, and flourish. Fair access additionally includes addressing spatial imbalances and differences in admittance to parks, green spaces, and sporting offices, guaranteeing that all occupants approach nature and open-air conveniences that advance wellbeing and prosperity. Furthermore, urban areas can advance financial incorporation by supporting independent companies, giving position-preparing and business-opening doors, and encouraging business among underserved networks.

Participatory dynamic cycles are fundamental for guaranteeing that metropolitan advancement choices are straightforward, responsible, and receptive to the requirements and needs of neighborhood inhabitants. By drawing in partners in the preparation, planning, and execution of tasks and drives, urban communities can construct trust, encourage joint effort, and create spaces where various points of view are esteemed and regarded. Participatory methodologies can take many forms, from public gatherings and studios to resident warning boards of trustees and online discussions, giving open doors to inhabitants to contribute their insight, ability, and lived encounters to the dynamic interaction. By enabling networks to have a voice in forming their future, urban communities can fabricate stronger, comprehensive, and manageable metropolitan conditions that mirror the necessities and yearnings, everything being equal.

All locally, commitment and social value are central standards of manageable metropolitan turn of events, offering pathways towards all the more strong and flourishing urban communities for all. By including networks in dynamic cycles, advancing social consideration and impartial access to assets and open doors, and cultivating participatory ways to deal with administration, urban communities can assemble more energetic, fair, and reasonable metropolitan conditions that upgrade personal satisfaction and prosperity, everything being equal.

Chapter 7: Consumer Choices and Green Lifestyles

Figuring out Shopper Conduct and its Ecological Effect

In the mind-boggling dance among organic markets, the decisions made by customers resonate a long way past the bounds of shopping paths and checkout counters; they shape the actual texture of our planet, impacting examples of asset utilization, squandering age, and ecological corruption on a worldwide scale. Understanding the multifaceted transaction between customer conduct and its ecological effect is fundamental for exploring the intricacies of current life and cultivating a more practical relationship with the normal world.

Shopper conduct incorporates a wide range of exercises, from buying choices and utilization examples to way of life decisions and social inclinations. At its center, shopper conduct mirrors the qualities, convictions, and needs of people and social orders, molding the interest in labor and products and driving monetary action across areas. In any case, customer conduct isn't exclusively determined by individual inclinations; it is additionally affected by outside elements, for example, promoting, accepted practices, peer strain, and market patterns, which can shape the view of significant worth, allure, and status.

The natural effect of shopper conduct is diverse and mind-boggling, incorporating a great many exercises and cycles all through the item lifecycle. From asset extraction and assembly to conveyance, utilization, and removal, each phase of the item lifecycle has ecological ramifications, from ozone-harming substance outflows and asset exhaustion to contamination and natural surroundings obliteration. Purchaser decisions can likewise drive interest in unreasonable practices like deforestation, overfishing, and annihilation of natural surroundings, fueling ecological corruption and compromising biodiversity and environmental administrations.

Understanding the natural effect of customer conduct requires a comprehensive point of view that thinks about the social, monetary, and environmental components of supportability. It includes inspecting the existence pattern of items and administrations, from unrefined substance extraction and creation to utilization and removal, and assessing the ecological and social results of each stage. It additionally involves perceiving the interconnectedness of human activities and their effects on environments, environment, and regular assets, and taking into account the more extensive foundational factors that shape customer conduct, like government strategies, corporate practices, and social standards.

By understanding the natural effect of purchaser conduct, people can make additional educated decisions that limit their environmental impression and advance manageability. This might include embracing practices, for example, diminishing utilization, picking items with lower natural effects, supporting eco-accommodating organizations, and pushing for strategies that advance maintainability and social obligation. At last, by adjusting our utilization propensities with our qualities and desires for a better, more reasonable future, we can bridle the force of customer conduct to drive positive change and make a reality where individuals and the planet flourish as one.

The Force of Cognizant Utilization

In the midst of the whirlwind of ads, advancements, and promoting messages that barrage us every day, there lies a calm, however strong, power—aa power that engages people to employ their buying power as a device for positive change. This power is cognizant utilization, a careful way to deal with shopping and utilization that focuses on natural supportability, social obligation, and moral contemplations. In our current reality, where buyer decisions convey critical weight, embracing cognizant utilization addresses a strong method for utilizing individual organizations to impact significant change and drive towards a more feasible future.

At its embodiment, cognizant utilization includes developing mindfulness and purposefulness in each buying choice, taking into account the quick advantages and expenses as well as the more extensive social, natural, and moral ramifications. It requires a shift away from careless utilization driven by motivation, comfort, or prevailing difficulty towards a more smart and intentional methodology that thinks about the drawn-out results of our activities. By turning out to be more cognizant buyers, we can adjust our buying propensities with our qualities and yearnings for a superior world, involving our wallets as a decision in favor of supportability, decency, and equity.

One of the vital parts of cognizant utilization is the act of informed direction, which includes investigating and figuring out the natural and social effects of items and organizations prior to making a purchase. This might include perusing item names, investigating brands and organizations, and searching out data from valid sources, for example, ecological associations, purchaser backing gatherings, and free affirmation plans. By outfitting ourselves with information and data, we can settle on additional educated decisions that mirror our qualities and needs, supporting organizations that focus on maintainability, straightforwardness, and moral strategic policies.

One more part of cognizant utilization is the development of careful utilization propensities, which includes being aware of our utilization examples and ways of behaving and going with intentional decisions to decrease squander, limit ecological effect, and advance supportability. This might include practices like diminishing, reusing, and reusing materials; picking items with negligible bundling or bundling that is recyclable or biodegradable; and keeping away from single-use things and disposables whenever the situation allows. By taking on a more careful way to deal with utilization, we can decrease our biological impression and contribute to the preservation of normal assets, the security of environments, and biodiversity.

Notwithstanding ecological contemplations, cognizant utilization additionally includes social and moral aspects, for example, supporting fair work rehearsals, common freedoms, and civil rights. This might include picking items that are delivered morally and economically, supporting organizations that give fair wages and safe working conditions for their representatives, and boycotting organizations that take part in untrustworthy or manipulative practices. By utilizing our buying ability to help organizations that maintain moral principles and contribute emphatically to society, we can advance civil rights and financial reasonableness and assist with making a more fair and only world for all.

At last, cognizant utilization isn't just about what we purchase; it's about how we decide to carry on with our lives and the qualities that we decide to maintain. By embracing cognizant utilization and pursuing decisions that line up with our qualities and goals for a superior world, we can tackle the force of buyer conduct to drive positive change and make a more manageable, impartial, and flourishing future for us and people in the future.

Economical shopping practices

In the clamoring commercial center of current life, each purchase we make conveys the possibility of shaping the eventual fate of our planet. Manageable shopping rehearsals offer a pathway towards lessening our ecological impression, advancing moral creation strategies, and supporting organizations that focus on friendly and natural obligation. By taking on careful and eco-cognizant shopping propensities, people can assume a critical role in driving positive change and adding to a more manageable and fair worldwide economy.

One of the foundations of reasonable shopping practices is the thought of an item's lifecycle and its natural effect. This includes assessing not just the materials and assembly processes used to deliver an item but additionally its transportation, bundling, and end-of-life removal. By picking items that are produced using sustainable or reused materials, fabricated utilizing eco-accommodating cycles, and bundled in negligible or recyclable bundling, purchasers can limit their biological impression and diminish their interest in assets and energy-serious creation techniques.

One more significant part of maintainable shopping practices is supporting organizations that focus on ecological manageability, social obligation, and moral strategic approaches. This might include searching out brands and organizations that have laid out responsibilities to manageability, for example, obtaining materials dependably, lessening ozone-harming substance discharges, and supporting fair work rehearsals. By supporting these organizations with our buying power, shoppers can boost the vast reception of economic practices and contribute to the progress towards a more maintainable and moral economy.

Picking privately created and natural items is one more key part of maintainable shopping rehearsals, as it decreases the ecological effect related to transportation and supports neighborhood economies and networks. Privately delivered merchandise normally requires fewer assets and creates fewer discharges during transportation, while natural items are developed without engineered pesticides, composts, or hereditarily changed creatures, advancing soil wellbeing, biodiversity, and environmental flexibility. By picking privately delivered and natural items whenever the situation allows, customers can uphold economical agribusiness practices and contribute to the conservation of normal biological systems and biodiversity.

Limiting waste and rehearsing mindful utilization are likewise fundamental for advancing manageability and decreasing ecological effects. This might include embracing practices, for example, purchasing just the thing that is required, staying away from drive-buys, and picking sturdy, excellent items that are intended to endure. Buyers can likewise diminish squander by fixing, reusing, or reusing things as opposed to discarding them, adding to the economy and limiting how much waste is shipped off landfills or incinerators.

Notwithstanding individual activities, aggregate endeavors and support assume a vital role in advancing economical shopping practices and driving foundational change towards a more maintainable and impartial economy. By supporting strategies and drives that advance straightforwardness, responsibility, and maintainability in the commercial center, shoppers can consider organizations and legislatures responsible for their natural and social effects and support an all-around and feasible future for all.

Generally speaking, maintainable shopping rehearsals offer a strong method for adjusting our customer conduct to our qualities and goals for a superior world. By making cognizant and eco-cognizant decisions in our regular purchases, we can contribute to the change towards a more maintainable, fair, and versatile worldwide economy that benefits both individuals and the planet.

Embracing green ways of life

In the embroidered artwork of our day-to-day existence, our propensities and schedules weave the strings of our reality, molding our singular encounters as well as the aggregate fate of our planet. Taking on green ways of life addresses a cognizant decision to embrace manageability, care, and ecological stewardship in each part of our lives, from the items we purchase and the food we eat to the manner in which we drive, devour energy, and cooperate with the normal world. By integrating supportable practices into our day-to-day schedules and propensities, we can lessen our natural impression, limit squandering, and contribute to a better, more manageable future for us and other people in the future.

One of the foundations of green ways of life is embracing sustainable and eco-accommodating practices in the home. This might include decreasing energy utilization by utilizing energy-productive machines, Drove lights, and brilliant indoor regulators, as well as protecting homes and fixing drafts to lessen warming and cooling costs. Green property holders may likewise focus on water preservation by introducing low-stream installations, water gathering frameworks, and dry-season safe finishing, as well as treating the soil as natural waste and reusing materials to limit squander shipped off landfills. By carrying out these practices, people can diminish their ecological effect and lower their service bills, setting aside cash while advancing manageability.

Green ways of life likewise encompass feasible transportation rehearsals, like strolling, cycling, carpooling, or involving public transportation, as options in contrast to driving alone in private vehicles. By picking dynamic transportation modes or imparting rides to other people, people can diminish ozone-harming substance emanations, air contamination, and gridlock, while likewise advancing actual work and working on general wellbeing. Green suburbanites may likewise consider switching to electric vehicles or hybrid vehicles controlled by sustainable power, further decreasing their carbon footprint and reliance on non-renewable energy sources.

One more part of green ways of life is embracing maintainable dietary propensities that focus on plant-based food sources, neighborhood and natural produce, and economical fish choices. By decreasing meat utilization and choosing plant-based proteins like beans, lentils, nuts, and tofu, people can diminish their carbon footprint, ration water, and alleviate deforestation related to creature farming. Green eaters may likewise uphold neighborhood rancher markets, local area upheld agribusiness (CSA) programs, and feasible food drives that advance harmless to the ecosystem cultivating rehearses and decrease food miles related to significant distance transportation.

Past individual activities, green ways of life likewise include drawing in with nature and upholding ecological preservation and manageability in our networks. This might include partaking in volunteer exercises, for example, tree planting, oceanside cleanups, or territory reclamation projects, as well as supporting natural associations and backing efforts that advance protection, environmental activity, and a maintainable turn of events. By interfacing with nature and becoming stewards of the climate, people can extend their obligation to manageability and move others to go along with them in making a more reasonable and versatile world for people in the future.

Eventually, taking on green ways of life isn't just about pursuing individual decisions; it's tied in with embracing an outlook of supportability, obligation, and stewardship that directs our activities and choices in each part of our lives. By embracing green ways of life and integrating supportable practices into our day-to-day schedules and propensities, we can show others how it is done, rouse others to make a move, and by and large work towards a more feasible, impartial, and flourishing future for all.

Aggregate Activity and Backing

In the orchestra of human undertakings, the force of aggregate activity and support resounds as an extraordinary power for driving fundamental shifts and molding the direction of history. In the domain of manageability, aggregate activity and backing assume a vital role in preparing networks, electrifying public help, and impacting strategies and practices that advance ecological protection, civil rights, and financial value. By combining efforts with similar people, associations, and developments, people can intensify their voices, influence their impact, and catalyze significant change on neighborhood, public, and worldwide scales.

One of the most intense types of aggregate activity is local area sorting out, which unites different partners, grassroots activists, and concerned residents to address normal difficulties and seek after shared objectives. Through people group sorting out endeavors like municipal events, grassroots missions, and alliance building, people can construct fortitude, cultivate coordinated effort, and activate assets to handle squeezing ecological issues, for example, environmental change, contamination, and territory obliteration. By coordinating aggregate activities like fights, energizes, and petitions, networks can bring issues to light, pressure chiefs, and request responsibility from state-run administrations, organizations, and different establishments.

Backing addresses one more amazing asset for driving change and advancing supportability, as it includes bringing issues to light, molding popular assessment, and impacting strategy choices through schooling, exceeding, and campaigning endeavors. Advocates for supportability might work with policymakers to create and execute regulations, guidelines, and drives that advance natural insurance, protection, and a reasonable turn of events. They may likewise take part in government-funded schooling efforts, media efforts, and virtual entertainment backing to bring issues to light about natural issues, activate public help, and gather speed for activity.

Notwithstanding group coordinating and promotion, aggregate activity can take numerous different forms, like cooperative drives, associations, and coalitions that unite assorted partners and assets to address complex supportability challenges. For instance, organizations, non-benefit associations, government offices, and local gatherings might team up on supportability undertakings like sustainable power establishments, squander decrease drives, or green foundation projects that benefit the climate and neighborhood networks. By pooling their aptitude, assets, and organizations, these cooperative endeavors can accomplish more noteworthy effects and make enduring change that benefits both individuals and the planet.

Fortitude and allyship are likewise fundamental parts of aggregate activity, as they include remaining in fortitude with underestimated networks, upholding their freedoms, and enhancing their voices while chasing after ecological equity and value. This might include supporting cutting-edge networks lopsidedly affected by natural contamination, environmental change, and social unfairness and pushing for strategies and drives that address foundational imbalances and advance comprehensive and impartial arrangements. By building coalitions across different networks and developments, people can cultivate fortitude, form power, and make an all-the-more manageable world for all.

At last, aggregate activity and support are fundamental mainstays of maintainability, offering pathways towards significant change and progress despite intricate and interconnected difficulties. By meeting up as people, networks, and social orders to request equity, value, and maintainability, we can bridle the force of aggregate activity to make a more splendid and economical future for us and people in the future.

Chapter 8: Policy and Governance for a Sustainable Future

Figuring out the job of strategy in maintainability

In the multifaceted dance of human progress, strategy fills in as the director, organizing the developments of society towards a reasonable future. At its embodiment, strategy addresses a bunch of rules, guidelines, and rules laid out by states to oversee conduct, designate assets, and address cultural difficulties. With regards to manageability, strategy assumes a basic role in forming the direction of ecological protection, social value, and the financial turn of events, giving the structure through which social orders explore the mind-boggling transaction between human exercise and the normal world.

The job of strategy in maintainability is multi-layered and broad, enveloping many issues and spaces, from ecological security and normal assets to social government assistance, general wellbeing, and financial administration. Ecological strategies, for instance, manage exercises such as contamination control, land use planning, biodiversity preservation, environmental change relief, planning to defend biological systems, safeguard regular assets, and moderate natural debasement. Social arrangements, then again, address issues like neediness, disparity, and social avoidance, trying to advance civil rights, common liberties, and fair access to assets and open doors.

Government strategies significantly affect cultural ways of behaving, impacting the decisions people, organizations, and foundations make in their regular routines and communications with the climate. By sanctioning regulations, guidelines, and motivations that advance reasonable practices and deter hurtful ways of behaving, policymakers can control social orders towards all the more harmless to the ecosystem, socially impartial, and financially strong pathways. For instance, strategies such as environmentally friendly power orders, carbon evaluating systems, and green structure guidelines can boost interest in clean energy, energy effectiveness, and practical foundations, diminish ozone-harming substance discharges, and advance feasible turn of events.

The viability of strategy in advancing maintainability relies upon different variables, including political will, institutional limits, partner commitment, and public help. Effective approaches are often the consequence of joint effort and agreement working among different partners, including government organizations, common society associations, organizations, and local gatherings. They are likewise educated by logical exploration, master examination, and partner input, guaranteeing that they are proof-based, attainable, and socially and politically satisfactory.

In the journey for manageability, strategy addresses both a test and an open door—aa test to conquer settled interests, political dormancy, and momentary reasoning—and a potential chance to catalyze groundbreaking change, encourage development, and fabricate a more practical and strong future for all. By perceiving the basic job of strategy in molding the circumstances for maintainability and upholding approaches that focus on ecological security, social value, and monetary thriving, people can contribute to the production of an all-the-more impartial and feasible world for the present and people in the future.

The Significance of Incorporated Arrangement Approaches

In the complicated embroidery of manageability, interconnectedness rules—an acknowledgment that ecological, social, and monetary difficulties are profoundly entwined and can't be tended to in segregation. Incorporated strategy approaches address a comprehensive and diverse reaction to these interconnected difficulties, recognizing the perplexing exchange between natural protection, social value, and the financial turn of events. By embracing coordinated strategy structures, legislatures can address manageability challenges in a thorough and composed way, advancing collaborations and keeping away from compromises between contending goals.

The significance of coordinated arrangement approaches lies in their capacity to rise above conventional storehouses and overcome any barrier between different areas, disciplines, and partners. As opposed to treating ecological, social, and financial issues as isolated and particular, coordinated strategies perceive their interconnectedness and try to address them in a brought-together and cognizant way. This includes separating institutional obstructions, cultivating joint effort among different partners, and taking on a framework-situated approach that considers the interdependencies and criticism circles between various parts of supportability.

Coordinated strategy moves toward likewise offering a pathway towards additional compelling and effective answers for supportability challenges by utilizing cooperative energies and keeping away from potentially negative side-effects. By tending to various elements of supportability at the same time, incorporated strategies can produce co-advantages and positive criticism circles that enhance their effect and make temperate patterns of progress. For instance, strategies that advance environmentally friendly power and energy proficiency not only lessen ozone-harming substance discharges and battle environmental change, but additionally make occupations, spike monetary development, and upgrade energy security.

Besides, incorporated strategy approaches can assist with tending to the main drivers of manageability challenges by handling fundamental drivers, for example, unreasonable utilization designs, unjust dispersion of assets, and impractical creation techniques. By taking on strategies that address these fundamental drivers, state-run administrations can create the circumstances for groundbreaking change and shift social orders towards additional reasonable and evenhanded directions. This might include taking on administrative measures, financial motivating forces, public speculations, and social projects that advance supportability, versatility, and inclusivity.

The execution of coordinated arrangements approaches serious areas of strength because it requires initiative, institutional limits, partner commitment to beat boundaries, and protection from change. It likewise requires hearty checking and assessment instruments to follow progress, recognize holes and open doors, and change arrangements and systems depending on the situation. By encouraging joint effort and association among legislatures, common society associations, organizations, and the scholarly community, incorporated strategy approaches can outfit the aggregate insight, assets, and skills of different partners to really address maintainability challenges and fabricate a stronger and evenhanded world for all.

All in all, coordinated strategy approaches are a useful asset for tending to the mind-boggling and interconnected difficulties of maintainability. By perceiving the reliance of natural, social, and financial issues and taking on comprehensive and complex arrangements, states can advance cooperative energies, stay away from compromises, and make a more supportable and fair future for the present and people in the future.

Advancing Manageable Improvement Objectives (SDGs)

In the journey for an additional feasible and impartial world, the Unified Countries Supportable Improvement Objectives (SDGs) stand as an encouraging sign—aa widespread source of inspiration to end neediness, safeguard the planet, and guarantee success for all. Taken on by world forerunners in 2015, the SDGs address a complete and coordinated system for tending to the interconnected difficulties of ecological manageability, social consideration, and the financial turn of events. Containing 17 objectives and 169 focuses, the SDGs give a guide to legislatures, organizations, common society, and people to cooperate towards a common vision of an all-the-more fair and reasonable future.

At the core of the SDGs lies a guarantee to abandon nobody—an acknowledgment that supportable improvement should be comprehensive and impartial and that the necessities and goals of the most helpless and underestimated populations should be focused on. The SDGs incorporate a great many interconnected issues, including neediness destruction, orientation balance, clean energy, environmental activity, reasonable urban communities, and biodiversity protection, mirroring the diverse idea of maintainability and the interdependencies between friendly, monetary, and ecological aspects.

Advancing the SDGs requires purposeful work to coordinate them into public and neighborhood strategy plans, systems, and dynamic cycles. This includes adjusting homegrown approaches, plans, and spending plans with the objectives and focuses of the SDGs, mainstreaming supportability contemplations into sectoral arrangements and projects, and laying out instruments for observing and investigating progress towards accomplishing the SDGs. By inserting the SDGs into public improvement plans and techniques, legislatures can flag their obligation to supportability and create a system for facilitating activity across various areas and levels of administration.

Common society associations, organizations, and different partners likewise play a significant role in advancing the SDGs and driving advancement towards their fulfillment. This might include bringing issues to light about the SDGs, assembling assets and organizations to help SDG execution, and considering legislatures and different partners responsible for their responsibilities and activities. By participating in support, effort, and cooperation, common society associations and organizations can enhance the effect of the SDGs and contribute to the accomplishment of shared objectives and targets.

Checking and following advancement towards the SDGs is fundamental for surveying the viability of approaches and mediations, distinguishing holes and difficulties, and directing endeavors to speed up progress. This requires hearty information assortment, investigation, and announcing frameworks that catch the full scope of social, monetary, and ecological pointers pertinent to the SDGs. By putting resources into the information foundation and limiting building drives, legislatures can improve their capacity to quantify progress, assess effect, and settle on proof-based choices to propel the SDGs.

At last, the outcome of the SDGs relies on the aggregate endeavors and responsibilities of states, organizations, common society, and people to cooperate for a typical reason. By embracing the standards and upsides of the SDGs, encouraging coordinated effort and organization among different partners, and making a strong and groundbreaking move, we can fabricate a more feasible, evenhanded, and prosperous world for the present and people in the future.

Carrying out green approaches and drives

Chasing a manageable future, the reception and execution of green strategies and drives arise as impetuses for extraordinary change, offering logical answers to address squeezing ecological diffi-culties and encouraging feasible turns of events. Green strategies include a different exhibit of measures pointed toward advancing ecological protection, decreasing fossil fuel byproducts, and cultivat-ing maintainable assets across different areas of society. These strat-egies and drives not only add to moderating environmental change and safeguarding biological systems, but additionally animate devel-opment, make green positions, and drive financial development in a way that is viable within planetary limits.

One of the vital mainstays of green strategies is the advancement of sustainable power and energy proficiency, which assumes an essential role in progressing towards a low-carbon economy and less-ening reliance on petroleum derivatives. Arrangements, for example, feed-in duties, environmentally friendly power commands, and duty motivations for clean energy speculations boost the sending of en-vironmentally friendly power advances, for example, solar, wind, hydro, and geothermal power. All the while, energy productivity guidelines, construction laws, and motivations for energy-proficient advancements and machines support energy preservation and di-minish energy utilization in structures, transportation, industry, and different areas.

Besides, green strategies reach beyond energy to encompass more extensive drives pointed toward advancing economic assets for ex-ecutives, squander decreases, and roundabout economy standards. Strategies like expanded maker obligation (EPR) programs, land-fill expenses, and restrictions on single-use plastics boost squander decrease, reusing, and the change towards a more roundabout economy, where assets are preserved, reused, and reused to limit squander and natural effects. Additionally, strategies that advance practical land use arranging, preservation agribusiness, and timber-land security add to biodiversity protection, soil wellbeing, and biological system versatility, while likewise alleviating deforestation, living space misfortune, and land debasement.

Notwithstanding natural contemplations, green strategies additionally focus on friendly value, consideration, and local area commitment, guaranteeing that the advantages of supportability are shared evenhandedly and that helpless and underestimated populations are not abandoned. This might include executing arrangements, for example, green work preparation programs, ecological equity drives, and local area-driven protection projects that engage nearby networks, advance social attachment, and upgrade strength to natural and financial shocks. By focusing on friendly value and consideration in green strategy making, legislatures can assemble support for maintainability drives and guarantee that they convey unmistakable advantages to all sections of society.

The effective execution of green approaches and drives areas of strength requires initiative, partner commitment, and institutional ability to defeat hindrances and protect against change. It likewise requires powerful checking, assessment, and authorization components to follow progress, recognize holes and amazing open doors, and consider legislatures and different partners responsible for their responsibilities and activities. By cultivating coordinated effort and association among legislatures, organizations, common society associations, and the scholarly community, green strategies can tackle the aggregate insight, assets, and skills of different partners to address supportability challenges successfully and fabricate a stronger and more fair world for the present and people in the future.

All in all, green strategies and drives address a useful asset for propelling manageability and encouraging a stronger, evenhanded, and prosperous future for all. By focusing on ecological preservation, carbon moderation, and feasible assets on the board while likewise advancing social value, consideration, and local area commitment, green strategies can drive extraordinary change and make a reality where individuals and the planet flourish as one.

Improving public interest and responsibility

In the popularity-based embroidered artwork of administration, public support and responsibility arise as fundamental strings, winding together the texture of maintainable strategy-making and administration. The dynamic commitment of residents, common society associations, and networks in the dynamic cycle is principal to guaranteeing that strategies and drives are receptive to the requirements, desires, and worries of the individuals they are planned to serve. Additionally, systems for straightforwardness, oversight, and responsibility are essential for considering legislatures and different partners responsible for their activities, guaranteeing that they maintain their responsibilities to manageability and follow through on their vows to the general population.

Public cooperation in the approach-creating cycle can take many forms, going from public conferences, official Q&A events, and resident gatherings to participatory planning processes, partner exchanges, and local area-based direction. By opening doors to significant commitment and discourse, state-run administrations can take advantage of the aggregate insight, information, and imagination of assorted partners, creating imaginative answers for complex manageability difficulties and building trust and authenticity in the dynamic cycle. Connecting with minimized and weak networks, specifically, is fundamental for guaranteeing that their voices are heard and their viewpoints are considered in approach detailing and execution.

Straightforwardness and responsibility instruments are fundamental for guaranteeing that state-run administrations and different partners are held liable for their activities and choices connected with manageability. This might include laying out systems for community access to data, like data regulations, open information drives, and online stages for sharing government information and archives. It might likewise include making autonomous oversight bodies, like review foundations, ombudsmen, and anti-defilement organizations, to examine grumblings, survey government activities, and consider authorities responsible for their lead.

Moreover, encouraging a culture of straightforwardness, honesty, and responsibility inside government organizations is urgent for advancing great administration and combating debasement, which can subvert manageability endeavors and disintegrate public confidence in government. This might include taking on measures like sets of principles for public authorities, irreconcilable situation guidelines, and informant security regulations to advance moral ways of behaving and respectability in open administration. It might likewise include fortifying legitimate systems and authorization instruments to arraign and rebuff demonstrations of debasement and impropriety.

Common society associations, media, and different guard dogs assume a basic role in considering legislatures and different partners responsible for their activities and upholding straightforwardness, responsibility, and great administration. By leading exploration, examinations, and promotion crusades, common society associations can shed light on defilement, maltreatment of force, and ecological infringement and prepare the public for changes and strategy changes. Likewise, free news sources and columnists assume an essential role in revealing bad behavior, uncovering debasement, and considering legislatures and other strong entertainers responsible for their activities.

At last, upgrading public support and responsibility in strategy making and administration is fundamental for propelling maintainability and building trust and authenticity in government establishments. By cultivating straightforwardness, commitment, and responsibility, legislatures can guarantee that strategies and drives are receptive to the necessities and desires of the individuals they serve and that they convey unmistakable advantages to society in general.

In doing so, they can create a more comprehensive, fair, and reasonable future for the present and people in the future.

Chapter 9: Education and Awareness: Empowering Change

The Job of Schooling in Maintainability

Schooling remains a foundation in the structure of manageability, filling in as both a reference point for edification and an impetus for extraordinary change. At its core, schooling engages people with the information, abilities, and values expected to comprehend, appreciate, and address the complicated difficulties confronting our planet. From homerooms to networks, instruction cultivates a more profound comprehension of the interconnectedness of social, financial, and natural frameworks, enlightening pathways towards an additional reasonable and evenhanded future.

The job of training in supportability stretches out a long way past the limits of conventional study halls, enveloping a wide range of formal and casual growth opportunities that lengthen the whole life expectancy. In proper schooling settings, like schools, colleges, and professional preparation programs, manageability training furnishes understudies with the apparatuses and points of view expected to

basically dissect maintainability issues, investigate creative arrangements, and take part in involved growth opportunities that advance dynamic citizenship and stewardship of the planet. Through
interdisciplinary methodologies that incorporate information from
different fields like science, social investigations, and morals, schooling develops an all-encompassing comprehension of maintainability
that rises above disciplinary limits and encourages framework thinking and critical thinking abilities.

Besides, schooling assumes an essential role in encouraging ecological proficiency—aa profound comprehension of the regular
world and the complicated interrelationships among people and
their current circumstances. Ecological education enables people to
pursue informed choices and make mindful moves that limit their
natural impression, ration regular assets, and safeguard biological
systems. By cultivating a feeling of association and stewardship towards the normal world, schooling supports a culture of ecological
obligation and supportability that saturates all parts of society.

Past advancing individual mindfulness and activity, training
likewise fills in as an impetus for more extensive cultural change, preparing networks, associations, and legislatures to focus on supportability in strategy making, arranging, and dynamic cycles. Through
group-based instruction drives, public mindfulness missions, and
backing endeavors, schooling gathers speed for aggregate activity and
motivates grassroots developments that drive extraordinary change
at neighborhood, public, and worldwide levels. By drawing in different partners in discourse, cooperation, and activity, schooling
cultivates a feeling of shared liability and aggregate responsibility for
challenges, making ripe ground for development, joint effort, and
good-friendly change.

All in all, training remains a strong power for propelling
manageability, enabling people and networks to become dynamic
problem solvers in building a more maintainable and fair world. By

encouraging decisive reasoning, ecological proficiency, and aggregate activity, training develops the information, abilities, and values expected to address the complicated difficulties confronting our planet and make a more promising time to come for the present and people in the future. As we leave on the excursion towards maintainability, schooling lights the way, directing our strides and moving us to take a stab at a reality where individuals and the planet flourish as one.

Advancing Ecological Education

In the midst of the embroidery of manageability, natural education arises as a directing light—aa reference point enlightening the way towards informed navigation, dependable stewardship, and aggregate activity notwithstanding ecological difficulties. Ecological education incorporates not just authentic information about environments, biodiversity, and regular cycles but also decisive reasoning abilities, values, and mentalities that move people to draw in with and care for the normal world. By advancing ecological proficiency, training furnishes people with the apparatuses and points of view expected to explore the intricacies of maintainability, pursue informed decisions, and advocate for positive change in their networks, among other things.

At its center, ecological proficiency is tied to figuring out the many-sided associations between human activities and the climate, perceiving the effects of human activities on biological systems, biodiversity, and regular assets, and valuing the worth of biodiversity, clean air, clean water, and other environmental benefits that support life on the planet. Ecological proficiency goes beyond simple consciousness of natural issues; it includes understanding the underlying drivers of natural issues, investigating their social, monetary, and political aspects, and investigating arrangements that advance natural supportability, civil rights, and financial thriving.

In conventional training settings, natural education is developed through interdisciplinary methodologies that coordinate information from different fields like science, biology, topography, financial matters, and social science. By drawing in understudies for active opportunities for growth, field trips, and outside training exercises, teachers can encourage a more profound association with nature and a feeling of obligation towards ecological stewardship. Through experiential learning, understudies foster decisive reasoning abilities, critical abilities to think, and a feeling of organization that enables them to make a move on natural issues and add to good change in their networks.

Besides, ecological proficiency stretches out past the study hall into casual learning conditions, for example, parks, galleries, nature focuses, and local area associations, where people, everything being equal, can take part in experiential learning, resident science projects, and natural promotion drives. By giving chances to active investigation, revelation, and cooperation, casual learning conditions supplement formal schooling endeavors and proposition important open doors for people to extend how they might interpret natural issues and foster functional abilities for tending to them.

As well as cultivating ecological proficiency among people, schooling assumes an essential role in building cultural limits with respect to tending to natural difficulties and advancing reasonable turns of events. By integrating ecological instruction into public strategy, arranging, and dynamic cycles, states can establish an empowering climate that supports informed direction, mindful asset management, and feasible improvement rehearsals. By putting resources into natural instruction programs, outreach drives, and public mindfulness crusades, states can bring issues to light about ecological issues, activate public help for maintainability drives, and gather speed for aggregate activity.

All in all, advancing ecological proficiency is fundamental for building an additional practical and versatile world where people, networks, and social orders flourish together as one with nature.

By developing a more profound comprehension of natural issues, cultivating decisive reasoning abilities, and engaging people to make a move, schooling lays the groundwork for a more maintainable future where individuals and the planet prosper together. As we endeavor to address the intricate difficulties confronting our planet, natural proficiency fills in as a directing compass, directing our endeavors and rousing us to make a reality where maintainability isn't simply an objective, but a lifestyle.

Cultivating Practical Ways of Life

In the midst of the maze of manageability, the development of practical ways of life arises as an encouraging sign—aa pathway towards orchestrating human prosperity with natural wellbeing and biological trustworthiness. Practical ways of life involve decisions and ways of behaving that limit biological impressions, save regular assets, and advance social value, cultivating a more adjusted and versatile connection among people and the planet. By encouraging mindfulness, understanding, and obligation to supportable living, instruction engages people to pursue informed decisions that add to a more reasonable future for them and for people in the future.

At its center, cultivating practical ways of life includes rethinking the manners by which we live, work, consume, and communicate with the normal world. It involves embracing propensities and practices that focus on asset proficiency, squander decrease, and natural stewardship, while additionally advancing human prosperity, social value, and social variety. Feasible ways of life incorporate a great many aspects, including transportation, lodging, food, clothing, relaxation exercises, and utilization designs, each offering potential open doors for people to settle on decisions that line up with their qualities and desires for a more supportable future.

Schooling assumes an urgent role in cultivating manageable ways of life by bringing issues to light about the effects of individual decisions and ways of behaving on the climate, society, and people in the future. By furnishing people with the information, abilities, and values expected to basically assess their utilization examples and ways of life, schooling engages them to pursue cognizant choices that limit their biological impression and advance manageability. Through experiential learning, pretending activities, and certifiable applications, training assists people with drawing an obvious conclusion regarding their own decisions and more extensive natural and social outcomes, rousing them to get a sense of ownership with their decisions and effectively partake in endeavors to fabricate a more manageable world.

Besides, training encourages a feeling of organization and strengthening among people, empowering them to imagine and seek after elective approaches to living that focus on supportability and prosperity over material utilization and financial development. By empowering inventiveness, advancement, and business venture, training supports the improvement of maintainable arrangements and practices that rock the boat and make ready for a more manageable future. Whether through economical plans, environmentally friendly power advancements, or regenerative horticulture rehearsals, instruction furnishes people with the abilities and certainty expected to contribute to positive change and shape the future they need to see.

As well as enabling people, training likewise assumes a crucial role in cultivating aggregate activity and local area commitment around maintainable living. By opening doors to cooperation, discourse, and friend learning, schooling makes spaces for people to share information, encounters, and best works, building interpersonal organizations and emotionally supportive networks that work with conduct change and aggregate activity. Through group-based drives, instructive missions, and grassroots developments, schooling prepares people, associations, and networks to cooperate towards shared objectives and goals for an additional practical and impartial world.

All in all, cultivating practical ways of life through schooling is fundamental for building an additional manageable and strong future where people, networks, and social orders flourish as one with nature. By equipping people with the information, abilities, and values expected to pursue informed decisions and make mindful moves, schooling engages them to become problem solvers in building a more maintainable world. As we endeavor to address the intricate difficulties confronting our planet, training fills in as a directing light, enlightening the way towards a future where manageability isn't simply an objective but rather a lifestyle.

Building Environment Versatility

In the turbulent scene of environmental change, building versatility arises as an encouraging sign—aa pathway towards adjusting to and moderating the effects of a changing environment while protecting the prosperity of networks and biological systems. Environment versatility envelops the limit of people, networks, and frameworks to expect, endure, recuperate from, and adjust to the unfriendly effects of environmental change, including outrageous climate occasions, rising ocean levels, moving precipitation designs, and other environment-related perils. Schooling assumes a critical role in building environmental strength by bringing issues to light about environmental change, encouraging versatile limits, and engaging networks to go to proactive lengths to lessen weakness and improve flexibility.

At its center, building environment versatility includes understanding the interconnected idea of environmental change and its effects on different parts of human culture and the climate. It involves perceiving the perplexing communications between environmental change and other social, financial, and ecological stressors, for example, neediness, disparity, land use change, and biological system debasement, and recognizing methodologies to address these interconnected difficulties in a comprehensive and coordinated way. By cultivating a more profound comprehension of environmental change science, effects, and transformation methodologies, schooling enables people and networks to pursue informed choices and go to proactive lengths to decrease their weaknesses and fabricate versatility for environment-related gambles.

Training likewise assumes a critical role in bringing issues to light about the significance of transformation and moderation estimates in answering environmental change. By furnishing people with the information, abilities, and devices expected to evaluate environment gambles, recognize transformation choices, and execute versatility building measures, schooling equips them with the ability to successfully respond to environment-related difficulties and limit their effects on lives and jobs. Through experiential learning, situation-arranging activities, and local area-based transformation projects, training encourages a culture of proactive risk management among executives and flexibility-building that empowers networks to expect and answer environment-related questions in an opportune and successful way.

Also, training advances environmental flexibility by encouraging versatile limits and enabling people and networks to adapt to and recuperate from environment-related shocks and stresses. By building abilities, for example, critical thinking, correspondence, collaboration, and authority, schooling upgrades people's capacity to answer evolving conditions, adjust to new conditions, and explore vulnerability notwithstanding environmental change. Through versatility-building exercises, for example, fiasco readiness preparation, biological system rebuilding projects, and economic vocation drives, training reinforces the flexibility of networks and environments, lessening weakness and improving versatile ability to environment-related gambles.

As well as building versatile limits at the individual and local area levels, schooling likewise assumes an urgent role in advancing environmental flexibility through strategy backing, local area commitment, and social preparation. By bringing issues to light about environmental change, pushing for strategy changes, and assembling public help for strength-building drives, instruction establishes an empowering climate for environmental activity and cultivates aggregate endeavors to address environment-related difficulties. Through associations with government offices, common society associations, and different partners, training enhances the effect of versatility-building endeavors and catalyzes extraordinary change at neighborhood, public, and worldwide scales.

All in all, building environmental versatility through schooling is fundamental to guaranteeing the prosperity and success of networks and biological systems, notwithstanding environmental change. By bringing issues to light, cultivating versatile limits, and engaging people and networks to go to proactive lengths to decrease weakness and upgrade strength, training assumes a basic part in building a more reasonable and strong future for all. As we defy the difficulties of an evolving environment, schooling fills in as an encouraging sign, directing our endeavors to fabricate an existence where networks flourish as one with nature, strong despite vulnerability and misfortune.

Preparing Youth Activity

In the unique scene of maintainability, youth arise as a considerable power for change—an age ready to lead the charge towards an additional, supportable, and versatile future. As inheritors of the planet, youth have a remarkable stake in the choices and activities taken today to address the difficulties of tomorrow. Schooling assumes a crucial role in preparing youth activity by enabling youngsters with the information, abilities, and inspiration expected to become viable problem solvers in building a more supportive world.

At its center, preparing youth activity includes tackling the energy, excitement, and innovativeness of youngsters to drive positive social and natural change. By giving open doors to youth to take part in significant growth opportunities, involved tasks, and authority improvement exercises, training supports a feeling of organization and strengthening among youngsters, empowering them to perceive their capability to have an effect in their networks and then some. Through experiential learning, mentorship projects, and youth-driven drives, training develops an age of changemakers who are enthusiastic about supportability and focused on making a move to resolve squeezing natural and social issues.

Besides, schooling encourages a feeling of interconnectedness and fortitude among youngsters, motivating them to cooperate towards shared objectives and yearnings for a more economical future. By cultivating coordinated effort, exchange, and aggregate activity, instruction makes spaces for youngsters to associate with similar friends, share thoughts, and activate assets to address normal difficulties. Through youth-driven associations, organizations, and developments, schooling intensifies the voices of youngsters and gives them stages to advocate for change, impact dynamic cycles, and drive groundbreaking activity at neighborhood, public, and worldwide levels.

Training likewise assumes a critical role in building the capacity of youngsters to address complex maintainability challenges and add to positive change in their networks. By giving open doors to expertise building, initiative turn of events, and metro commitment, instruction outfits youngsters with the apparatuses and capabilities expected to distinguish issues, foster inventive arrangements, and carry out effective tasks that address squeezing natural and social issues. Through active growth opportunities, temporary positions, and volunteer open doors, schooling engages youngsters to apply their insight and abilities in true settings, acquiring useful experience and putting forth significant commitments to practical improvement attempts.

Besides, schooling encourages a culture of long-lasting learning and persistent improvement among youngsters, rousing them to remain educated, connected with, and dynamic in tending to supportability challenges all through their lives. By advancing decisive reasoning, interest, and receptiveness, training urges youngsters to scrutinize business as usual, challenge the customary way of thinking, and investigate alternative viewpoints and answers for complex issues. Through continuous learning open doors, mentorship connections, and friend-encouragement groups of people, instruction sustains a feeling of flexibility and versatility among youngsters, empowering them to explore vulnerability and change with certainty and good faith.

All in all, preparing youth activity through schooling is fundamental for building an additional supportable and versatile future where youngsters are engaged to contribute their gifts, energy, and imagination to tending to ecological and social difficulties. By encouraging a feeling of organization, fortitude, and long-lasting learning among youngsters, schooling develops an age of changemakers who are focused on building a reality where individuals and the planet flourish as one. As we face the intricate difficulties of manageability, schooling fills in as an impetus for trust, moving youngsters to think beyond practical boundaries, make a strong move, and shape a more promising time to come for them and for a long time into the future.

Chapter 10: Towards a Greener Future

Defining Aggressive Objectives for Supportability

In the mission for a greener future, the excursion starts with the definition of aggressive objectives—aa guide that directs our aggregate endeavors towards accomplishing supportability in the entirety of its aspects. Aggressive objectives act as signals of desire, energizing people, networks, and countries around shared dreams of an additional, reasonable, and fair world. By articulating clear targets and timetables for activity, aggressive objectives give structure to estimating progress, stirring activity, and considering partners responsible for their responsibilities to supportability.

At the core of defining aggressive objectives lies the acknowledgement of the earnestness and extent of the natural and social difficulties we face. From environmental change and biodiversity misfortune to asset consumption and social disparity, the size of the emergencies going up against our planet requires strong and conclusive activity. Aggressive objectives challenge us to think beyond the same old thing, pushing the limits of what is conceivable and moving development, innovativeness, and joint effort on a world-wide scale.

In addition, aggressive objectives act as impetuses for extraordinary change, igniting shifts in attitude, conduct, and strategy that are fundamental for achieving maintainability. By articulating striking dreams representing things to come, we try to make aggressive objectives that motivate trust, ingrain certainty, and assemble support for change among different partners. They give a revitalizing cry to legislatures, organizations, common society associations, and people to meet up, pool their assets, and work towards normal targets in quest for a common vision of maintainability.

Laying out aggressive objectives additionally requires careful consideration of the interconnections between the natural, social, and monetary components of supportability. Aggressive objectives should be all-encompassing and incorporated, tending to the underlying drivers of maintainability challenges and advancing collaborations and co-benefits across various areas and spaces. They should likewise be fair and comprehensive, guaranteeing that the advantages of supportability are shared evenhandedly and that powerless and underestimated populations are not abandoned.

As well as articulating long-term dreams of manageability, aggressive objectives additionally require concrete and noteworthy targets and achievements to direct execution and screen progress. These objectives ought to be science-based, proof-driven, and informed by the most ideal that anyone could hope to find information and ability. They ought to be aggressive yet feasible, moving partners to extend past their usual ranges of familiarity while likewise giving a practical pathway to progress.

All in all, defining aggressive objectives for supportability is fundamental for driving advancement towards a greener future. By articulating striking dreams, cultivating coordinated effort, and activating activity across areas and social orders, aggressive objectives move trust and catalyze extraordinary change. As we outline a course towards an additional reasonable and evenhanded world, aggressive objectives act as directing stars, enlightening the way forward, and rousing us to go after the most elevated yearnings of human potential and planetary prosperity.

Embracing advancement and innovation

Chasing a greener future, development and innovation arise as strong partners, offering groundbreaking answers for probably the most squeezing ecological and social difficulties within recent memory. Embracing advancement involves outfitting the force of human imagination, creativity, and innovation to foster better approaches for living, working, and interfacing with the normal world that are more practical, versatile, and impartial. Innovation, in the meantime, fills in as an empowering agent, giving the apparatuses, stages, and framework expected to make an interpretation of imaginative thoughts into substantial arrangements that can drive progress towards supportability.

At its center, embracing development and innovation includes embracing a mentality of interest, trial and error, and ceaseless improvement—an eagerness to shake things up and investigate additional opportunities for tending to maintainability challenges. This attitude is established in the acknowledgment that the arrangements of the past may not get the job done for the difficulties representing things to come and that new methodologies and advancements might be expected to conquer boundaries and open doors for progress.

Development and innovation offer plenty of chances for propelling maintainability across different areas and spaces. From environmentally friendly power and clean transportation to maintainable farming and round economy rehearsals, imaginative advancements are altering customary enterprises and opening up new pathways towards more feasible and productive asset use. For instance, propels in sustainable power innovations, such as sunlight-based, wind-based, and hydroelectric power, are driving progress towards a low-carbon energy framework, lessening ozone-harming substance emanations, and relieving the effects of environmental change.

Also, development and innovation hold the commitment of democratizing access to manageable arrangements, making them more available, reasonable, and adaptable for networks all over the planet. From off-lattice solar-powered chargers and portable financial administrations to minimal-cost water cleansing frameworks and 3D-printed lodging, creative innovations can possibly engage people and networks to meet their essential necessities while additionally diminishing their natural impression. By utilizing the force of advanced advancements like the web, cell phones, and remote detecting, imaginative arrangements can arrive at even the most remote and minimized populaces, connecting holes in access to fundamental administrations and enabling individuals to fabricate stronger and more supportable occupations.

Besides, embracing development and innovation requires cultivating a culture of joint effort, co-creation, and information sharing between different partners, including states, organizations, research establishments, common society associations, and nearby networks. By separating storehouses and advancing interdisciplinary cooperation, partners can use their aggregate skills, assets, and organizations to speed up the speed of advancement and scale up effective arrangements. Open advancement stages, hackathons, and development provokes offer significant open doors for partners to meet up, trade thoughts, and co-plan arrangements that address shared difficulties and make shared incentives for society.

All in all, embracing development and innovation is fundamental for driving advancement towards a greener future. By tackling the forces of human inventiveness, creativity, and innovation, we can foster groundbreaking arrangements that address the perplexing difficulties of maintainability and make a more prosperous, impartial, and strong world for the present and people in the future. As we set out on this excursion, let us embrace development as a power for good, tackling the force of innovation to fabricate a more splendid, more maintainable future for all.

Cultivating cooperation and organization

Chasing a greener future, joint effort and organization arise as foundations of progress, offering pathways to intensify influence, influence assets, and address complex supportability challenges all the more. Encouraging cooperation includes developing connections and organizations among different partners, including state-run administrations, organizations, common society associations, the scholarly world, and neighborhood networks, to cooperate towards shared objectives and goals. In the meantime, organization involves producing key partnerships and alliances that bridle the aggregate qualities and aptitudes of various entertainers to drive aggregate activity and make positive change.

At its embodiment, encouraging cooperation and organization requires an outlook of receptiveness, trust, and common regard—an acknowledgment that no single association or area can address supportability challenges in detachment and that significant advancement requires aggregate exertion and shared liability. This outlook is grounded in the comprehension that every partner brings novel viewpoints, assets, and capacities to the table and that by cooperating, we can accomplish more prominent effects and manageable results than by acting alone.

Joint efforts and organization offer various advantages for propelling supportability across different areas and spaces. By pooling assets, sharing information, and adjusting endeavors, partners can accomplish economies of scale and degree, diminishing duplication of endeavors and augmenting the proficiency and adequacy of intercessions. In addition, coordinated effort empowers partners to use correlative qualities and abilities, taking advantage of one another's organizations, abilities, and assets to address complex difficulties all the more thoroughly and comprehensively.

Besides, coordinated effort and association work with development and innovativeness by cultivating cross-preparation of thoughts, points of view, and approaches. By uniting assorted partners with various foundations, encounters, and skills, coordinated effort sets out open doors for learning, trial and error, and co-creation, prompting the advancement of inventive arrangements that might not have been imaginable through individual endeavors alone. Through cooperative examination, pilot ventures, and information trade stages, partners can outfit the force of aggregate knowledge to handle supportability challenges all the more successfully and create new experiences and arrangements.

Besides, coordinated effort and organization are fundamental for building trust, authenticity, and a social permit for maintainability drives. By drawing in partners in discourse, conferences, and dynamic cycles, cooperation guarantees that different voices and points of view are heard and regarded, fabricating agreement and purchasing in for shared objectives and goals. Besides, cooperation encourages responsibility and straightforwardness by making components for checking, assessment, and covering progress, considering partners responsible for their responsibilities and activities towards manageability.

All in all, cultivating cooperation and organization is fundamental for driving advancement towards a greener future. By outfitting the force of aggregate activity, partners can accomplish more noteworthy effects, advancements, and flexibility in tending to maintainability challenges. As we cooperate towards shared objectives and goals, let us embrace coordinated effort as a foundation of progress, producing organizations that rise above limits and make positive change for individuals and the planet.

Enabling people and networks

At the core of the excursion towards a greener future lies the strengthening of people and networks—aa cycle that cultivates organization, fabricates limits, and catalyzes grassroots activity in quest for supportability. Enabling people involves furnishing them with the information, abilities, assets, and valuable open doors expected to partake genuinely in dynamic cycles, make a move on supportability issues, and add to positive change in their networks and then some. Also, engaging networks includes building their aggregate ability to distinguish needs, put forth objectives, and carry out arrangements that address neighborhood manageability challenges and work on personal satisfaction for inhabitants.

Strengthening starts with training—an establishment whereupon people and networks can construct how they might interpret supportability issues, foster decisive reasoning abilities, and develop a feeling of organization and obligation towards the climate and society. By giving admittance to quality training, including ecological and manageability schooling, people can procure the information and abilities expected to go with informed choices, embrace supportable ways of behaving, and advocate for change in their networks. Schooling likewise assumes a critical role in bringing issues to light about ecological equity, social value, and common freedoms, enabling people to perceive and address foundational disparities and treacheries that propagate natural debasement and social underestimation.

In addition, strengthening includes furnishing people and networks with access to assets and potential open doors that empower them to make a move on manageability issues. This might include admittance to subsidizing, specialized help, preparing projects, and encouraging groups of people that help people and networks create and carry out manageable answers for neighborhood challenges. By putting resources into grassroots drives, local area-driven ventures, and limit-building programs, partners can enable people and networks to become dynamic problem solvers, driving advancement towards maintainability from the bottom up.

Besides, strengthening requires creating spaces and stages for significant cooperation and commitment where people and networks can voice their interests, express their desires, and contribute their plans to dynamic cycles that influence their lives and livelihoods. Participatory methodologies, like local gatherings, resident discussions, and participatory planning processes, empower partners to team up, co-plan, and co-execute arrangements that reflect nearby needs and values. By cultivating a culture of inclusivity, regard, and discourse, strengthening guarantees that different voices are heard and esteemed, prompting more impartial and economical results for all.

Moreover, strengthening includes encouraging authority and city commitment among people and networks, empowering them to assemble assets, construct alliances, and advocate for change on manageability issues. By opening doors to administration improvement, mentorship, and systems administration, partners can engage arising pioneers to become bosses of supportability in their networks and then some. Through grassroots getting sorted out, backing efforts, and local area activism, engaged people and networks can enhance their voices, impact leaders, and drive groundbreaking change at neighborhood, public, and worldwide levels.

All in all, enabling people and networks is fundamental for driving advancement towards a greener future. By putting resources into training, access to assets, participatory cycles, and initiative turns of events, partners can release the capability of people and networks to become dynamic problem solvers in building an additional, maintainable, and evenhanded world. As we set out on this excursion, let us perceive the force of strengthening to catalyze grassroots activity and make positive change for individuals and the planet.

Guaranteeing an Impartial and Comprehensive Turn of Events

Chasing a greener future, it is basic to focus on an impartial and comprehensive turn of events—aa promise to guarantee that manageability drives benefit all citizens, especially the individuals who are generally helpless and underestimated. Fair and comprehensive advancement involves addressing variations in access to assets, valuable open doors, and dynamic cycles, and advancing civil rights, common freedoms, and pride for all. By setting value and incorporation at the focal point of maintainability endeavors, partners can make stronger, firmer, and more prosperous networks where everybody has the chance to flourish.

At its center, guaranteeing impartial and comprehensive advancement requires perceiving and tending to fundamental disparities and treacheries that sustain natural corruption and social prohibition. This remembers aberrations for money, abundance, schooling, medical services, lodging, and admittance to clean air, water, and green spaces, which excessively influence underestimated networks, including low-paying families, native people groups, ladies, kids, people with incapacities, and ethnic minorities. By embracing a civil rights focal point, partners can distinguish and address the main drivers of disparity and treachery, guaranteeing that manageability drives advance decency, nobility, and basic liberties for all.

In addition, guaranteeing fair and comprehensive advancement includes elevating participatory ways to deal with dynamics that engage underestimated networks to voice their interests, articulate their requirements, and shape the results of maintainability drives that influence their lives and vocations. This might include drawing in networks for arranging processes, leading effect appraisals, and carrying out projects as a team with neighborhood partners, guaranteeing that their points of view and needs are considered and that advantages are conveyed fairly. By cultivating discourse, trust, and cooperation, partners can fabricate organizations with underestimated networks in view of common regard, fortitude, and shared responsibility for endeavors.

Moreover, guaranteeing impartial and comprehensive advancement requires putting resources into designated mediations and certifiable activities that address the particular necessities and weaknesses of minimized gatherings and advance their full cooperation and consideration in the public arena. This might incorporate giving admittance to training, medical care, social insurance, and financial open doors, as well as agreed measures to advance orientation fairness, enable native people groups, and support the privileges of underestimated networks. By tending to underlying boundaries and advancing social incorporation, partners can establish empowering conditions that empower underestimated gatherings to understand their maximum capacity and add to the practical turn of events.

Furthermore, guaranteeing impartial and comprehensive improvement includes advancing ecological equity—aa pledge to tend to natural imbalances and guaranteeing that all networks approach a perfect, sound, and economical climate. This incorporates tending to natural contamination, tainting, and debasement in minimized networks, as well as advancing local area-based arrangements that engage impacted networks to safeguard their wellbeing and climate. By upholding more grounded ecological guidelines, implementing natural regulations, and supporting local area drives, partners can progress ecological equity and guarantee that no local area is abandoned in the transition to a greener future.

All in all, guaranteeing fair and comprehensive improvement is fundamental for driving advancement towards a greener future that abandons nobody. By focusing on value, consideration, and civil rights in maintainability endeavors, partners can fabricate stronger, durable, and prosperous networks where everybody has the chance to flourish. As we endeavor to make an additional reasonable and impartial world, let us focus on maintaining the standards of value

and incorporation and cooperating to address fundamental disparities and treacheries that propagate natural corruption and social
prohibition.